D1491524

SPEAK

First published in October 2020

British Library Cataloguing in Publication Data
A catalogue record for this book is available
from the British Library.

ISBN 978 1 78521 699 2
Library of Congress catalog card no. 2019950894

Published by J H Haynes & Co. Ltd.,
Sparkford, Yeovil, Somerset BA22 7JJ, UK
Tel: 01963 440635
Int. tel: +44 1963 440635
Website: www.haynes.com

Haynes North America Inc.
859 Lawrence Drive, Newbury Park,
California 91320, USA

Printed and bound in Malaysia

While every effort is taken to ensure the accuracy of the
information given in this book, no liability can be accepted
by the author or publishers for any loss, damage or injury
caused by errors in, or omissions from the information given.

AUTHOR'S ACKNOWLEDGEMENTS
There are so many people to thank, but please bear with me because
encouragement and inspiration is really important when you are writing
a book, as it can be a lonely road. I would like to thank my brilliant family
and friends for all their help and encouragement; my children Leonie
and Oliver, my son-in-law Francois and daughter-in-law Luci, and
grandchildren Sasha, Pierre, Raphaelle, Harry, Ben and Matilda.

Thanks too to William Hanson, Jo Wheeler, Maureen Oakden and Kim
Dewdney for their time and invaluable contributions. Joanne Rippin at
Haynes and my editor Lucy Doncaster for their advice. And to my agent
Charlotte Howard at Fox Howard who is always so great in coming up
with new opportunities, Emma Jaffray for her ideas and thoughtful,
honest feedback and Fi Midwood for her unwavering support.
And finally thanks to Ian for the joy he has brought into my life.

SPEAK

ALL YOU NEED TO KNOW IN ONE CONCISE MANUAL

Haynes

Diana Mather

Contents

Introduction		**7**
First things to consider		**11**
	Why you?	12
	Who do they think you are?	12
	Why are you giving this talk?	12
	What do you need to know before you write the talk?	13
	What do you want the talk to achieve?	13
	How can you use your talk to achieve its aim?	14
	Are you the only speaker?	15
	Are you the keynote speaker?	15
	At what time are you speaking and for how long?	15
	Who else is speaking and what are their topics?	16
	Where is the venue?	17
	Is there a fee?	17
The audience		**19**
	Who is the audience?	20
	What size is the audience?	21
	What age is the audience?	21
	What do they want to know?	21
	What do they know already?	22
	What are their jobs or positions?	22
	Audience breakdown	22
	Who are the key people in the audience?	23
Creation		**25**
	Opening remarks and introduction	27
	Key words and key points	28
	Visual language	29
	The conclusion	33
	Tricks of the trade	33
Preparation		**35**
	Write, read, record	37
	Scripted talks	37
	How to practise effectively	38
	Tailoring your speech to the event	40
Visual aids and how to use them effectively		**55**
	Traditional visuals	56
	PowerPoint, Keynote and Prezi	56
	Whiteboards	62
	Flipcharts	62
	Video	63
	Audio	63
	Handouts	63

Using your voice and body   **65**

How to speak clearly   67

Why body language is important   71

Body talk   71

Conquering nerves   **79**

What makes us nervous?   80

Don't bottle out!   82

Living with your nerves   84

Understanding your nerves   84

Exercises to help banish nerves   86

Creating confidence   **89**

Positive thinking   90

Believe in yourself   93

Don't confuse memory with facts   93

False confidence   93

How to create confidence before the presentation   95

How to maintain confidence while speaking   97

First impressions   98

You are what you wear   99

Hair and make-up   103

Performance   **105**

Introduce yourself if no introduction has been made   106

Where and how to stand   106

Find your physical focus   107

Wait for the audience to become quiet   109

Look at the audience   111

Put passion into your presentation   111

Use your voice   111

Taking questions   113

How to cope in adverse situations   114

Summary and quick tips   **117**

Common errors   118

Before you agree to give a talk, ask these questions: 119

What do you want the talk to achieve?   119

Who are your audience?   119

Creation audit   119

Performance audit   120

Performance tips   120

How your body talks   121

Confidence checklist   123

Banishing nerves   123

Index   **126**

Introduction

*'Nothing great was ever achieved
without enthusiasm'*

Ralph Waldo Emerson

Public speaking is something that many
people dread, but it is something most of
us have to do at some time in our lives.
I am lucky that it has never really been a
bugbear for me and I have always been
reasonably happy to stand up and speak.
However, that doesn't mean that I don't get
nervous, or that I don't understand and
sympathise with people who find it difficult
or even terrifying. The aim of this book is
to show you how to get rid of your fear and
embrace the chance to speak to an
audience and get your point across.

Going to drama and ballet school taught me some important things about speaking in public. The rigorous training was brilliant, showing me how to use my voice and my body to express myself. What's more, those old clichés – getting into character by pretending to be a cat or standing stock still imagining I was a tree – helped me to get rid of inhibitions and stopped me worrying about making a fool of myself. For me, getting into character starts with the shoes and the walk; to conquer my nerves, I wear a pair of my favourite shoes and walk like a confident celebrity. I have found this tactic very useful, especially when I feel a bit daunted, such as when I'm facilitating at a conference or speaking to a large audience. I was also taught to use my body to express emotions. This is really important, and something that actors and speakers sometimes forget to do. For

The power of speech

From as far back as the ancient Egyptians, words have been synonymous with magic and immortality. In fact, the word 'spell' meant 'utterance'. This meant that while the written word carried authority, to make the magic effective the words had to be spoken out loud.

instance, I remember a time when the principal at the drama and ballet school was particularly frustrated with our lack of progress when rehearsing a play and said to us 'the ballet students have more acting talent in their little fingers than you actors have in your whole bodies!' That made us pull our socks up and re-evaluate our performances, I can tell you.

Preparation and practice are also critical to good performance. Actors always worry about forgetting lines or their voices drying up, but thankfully it very rarely happens because they prepare and rehearse thoroughly. You have to do the same if you want to be an inspiring speaker.

If I had to choose two things that mark out great speakers, they would be 1) enthusiasm and 2) a strong, clear message. But is your audience hearing the right message – the message you want them to hear? This book will tell you how to ensure your message is received in the way you want it to be. What's more, it will show you how to inspire, motivate and entertain, and how to carry your audience with you on a wave of enthusiasm – whomever you are speaking to. To this end, the voice, body language, technology and, of course, content will also be discussed in detail throughout the forthcoming chapters, in relation to a wide spectrum of different situations. So, whether you are speaking at a wedding, an anniversary or a global conference, there is something here for you.

Moving with the times

Oratory is an age-old tradition, but in recent times technology has had a dramatic effect on how we can and should present our information to our audience. For example, there are many more global presentations nowadays, which may mean that we have to speak through an interpreter – an art form in itself that necessitates a different way of writing and delivering a speech. There are also more 'remote' presentations, made using technology such as Skype, and these require you to master a different kind of performance. Even if you are presenting your talk in a more conventional setting and manner, technology has moved on so much that people now expect a faster, more exciting experience; your audience will demand something visual – and I don't mean a simple PowerPoint presentation. Clever use of video and high-quality images as well as text is what is needed. All of this requires adequate preparation and an understanding of the audience's requirements – topics that we will cover in detail later in the book.

Chapter 1

First things to consider

'There are always three speeches, for every one you actually gave. The one you practiced, the one you gave, and the one you wish you gave.'

Dale Carnegie

You will probably end up giving a speech at some time in your life, but you may well dread the very thought of it. The vast majority of people rank public speaking as their number 1 fear, according to the National Institutes of Mental Health. This is odd, because we speak to people daily, but there is definitely something about standing up in front of others that makes speaking in public a nerve-wracking experience.

To help you prepare and give the best performance you can, there are some questions you should ask yourself next time you are asked to speak in public.

Why you?

'Why me?' is the question you should ask before you accept an invitation to speak or start to write any talk. You need to make sure that you are the right person to speak at that event and it is you and your experience and expertise that they want. So, why have you been asked to speak? There could be many reasons: you could be the expert in your field, you could have a reputation as a very amusing speaker, or you could be the only person who said 'yes'. Find out which it is and check that you agree and are happy to continue.

Who do they think you are?

It sounds obvious but you should make sure you are the person they think you are and are able to speak on the subject they want you to speak on. People share names, and there is scope for confusion. For instance, at one time there were three Peter Wheelers connected with BBC TV. One was a rugby player and commentator, another a broadcaster and the third was a technician. Peter Wheeler the rugby player and Peter Wheeler the broadcaster were both on the public speaking circuit and it was surprising how often they nearly got mixed up.

Why are you giving this talk?

Are you giving this talk to inform, amuse, sell, motivate, persuade or to shake people up a bit? We must always have a reason for giving a talk, so decide what you want from it and what you want the audience to do as a result. Sometimes the reason is

obvious, such as if you are father of the bride and speaking at your daughter's wedding. Non-professional speeches such as this are usually more easily defined according to the occasion, be it a celebration, funeral or at a club of some kind. I will be covering this in greater detail later. Professional speeches may have a less clear purpose, and it pays to take the time to clarify your intention and that of the people who have hired you.

What do you need to know before you write the talk?

Before you take on the task of giving a talk, it is important to ascertain three key facts:

- ■ The subject
- ■ The purpose or objective
- ■ The audience

What do you want the talk to achieve?

Having confirmed the basics, you now need to establish the purpose of the talk. Do you want to:

- ■ Inform?
- ■ Influence?
- ■ Inspire?
- ■ Sell?
- ■ Motivate?
- ■ Entertain?

Before starting to write a speech, it can be helpful to note down in a sentence what message you want your audience to take away with them. This will help to clarify your thoughts, cut down on the waffle and make your objective clear. For example:

What is your Story?

- 'To inform the board that resources spent on recruitment services will ensure we find the right person for the job.'
- 'To convince the members that it would save the Club money if we were to buy all our drinks from one supplier.'

How can you use your talk to achieve its aim?

Because you are telling a story, the words you use are critical in making that story attention-grabbing, motivating and compelling. In 1967, Albert Mehrabian – a

> *'Words have incredible power. They can make people's hearts soar, or they can make people's hearts sore.'*
>
> **Dr Mardy Grothe**

Professor Emeritus at the University of California – claimed that:

- 7 per cent of the effectiveness of communication is down to language
- 38 per cent hinges on the tone of voice
- 55 per cent is down to body language

In fact, though, Professor Mehrabian's research has been misconstrued. His experiments were mainly aimed at discovering how *emotions* are communicated. Indeed, he is so sick of being misunderstood and misapplied that his website has a paragraph imploring people not to do so. Obviously, tone of voice and body language are hugely important, but *what* we say, not just *how* we say it, really matters. This is especially true if people are going to read a copy of your speech. If you want to motivate and inspire your audience, to change beliefs and behaviours, the stories you create and the words you use must paint pictures and weave spells. It doesn't matter how 'dry' that subject might be, there is always a way to inject some magic. The question is, are you able to do that?

What you say obviously depends on the event and why you have been asked to speak. If the event is work-related you will have a good idea of what the audience is expecting, whereas if you are there as the 'entertainment' you can choose the topic you are most happy with, provided that you have done your research and have established the make-up of your audience. Professionally, you will probably be asked to fill 45 minutes to an hour. An hour is quite a long time, especially in this age of shrinking concentration spans. Will your material fill an hour? If not, speak for as long as the material allows and then ask for questions. Not many people complain about a speech being too short, especially at weddings and parties, so don't feel you have to pad things out.

Are you the only speaker?

If you are the only speaker you have it all to do. This means that you are the star of the show, especially if you are speaking at a family celebration. This can be quite daunting, but it does have the advantage

that you are not going to be overshadowed by other speakers and don't have to worry about repetition.

Are you the keynote speaker?

At a conference, if you are the keynote speaker you should be given the prime and longest slot. You will have been asked to speak because of your knowledge, your expertise and your experience and the audience will be primed to hear everything you know, so it is important to live up to their expectations. Again, you are the star of the show so you and your data, ideas and facts will be under the spotlight. This means that preparation has to be extremely thorough and it is important to rehearse the speech as much as possible – preferably 12 times. There is more on this in Chapter 4.

At what time are you speaking and for how long?

The length of time you are expected to speak for will affect the amount of material you can present. The time of the speech will also dictate your content and your performance. If, when speaking at a

Props

The use of screens, video, music, demos, and props all help to keep your audience alert and awake. TED (Technology, Entertainment and Design) was originally a conference devoted purely to technology, entertainment and design. It is now a worldwide phenomenon. There are millions of hits on thousands of TED Talks which are uploaded onto the net nearly every day.

Chris Anderson, Head of TED and Head Curator talks about the use of props in his book, 'TED Talks, the Official TED Guide to Public Speaking'. He says, 'Numerous TED Talks have been elevated by the use of unexpected props. To make a point about left and right brain hemispheres, Jill Bolte Taylor brought a real human brain onto the stage, complete with dangling spinal column.'

I don't recommend most of us to go that far, but you can see how the use of props can make an impact! In these days of data deluge, something physical that shocks, surprises or jolts us out of our comfort zone can be very effective.

full-day conference, you are one of the first on, the audience will be fresh and eager to listen. This is generally the case throughout the morning until lunch break, when some people might begin suffering from information overload. So, as you get towards midday it is best to keep your talk as succinct as possible if you want to retain attention. The most difficult time is just after lunch, often known as the 'graveyard' slot, when some people may feel a bit sleepy. In order to combat this and ensure you will be heard and appreciated the presentation has to be as lively and as interactive as possible.

Who else is speaking and what are their topics?

This will have a bearing on the information you deliver since you don't want to repeat what has come before or drift into someone else's subject matter. This can happen in particular at retirement parties. Again, talking to the other speakers and finding out what they will cover beforehand will allow you to prepare and target your talk for that particular event and that particular audience.

Timekeeping

It is vital to keep within your allotted time. If you run over it means someone else has less time, or the whole event overruns – something the organisers will not be happy about, especially the caterers if mealtimes run late. This is particularly true at weddings and big celebrations, where meals can be ruined if the speeches go on too long. Again, adequate preparation and practice are essential.

Where is the venue?

Obviously, the venue is important. Where is it, what size is it and how will you get there? Finding the best route is important so that you arrive cool and unflustered. You should get there in plenty of time as this will allow you to get yourself organised, check equipment and go over your speech. It will also help to calm the nerves of the organisers; having a speaker who is late or, worse still, doesn't turn up at all, is a complete nightmare for them.

Having worked out where the gig is to take place, there are still more questions to ask about the venue. Should you take your laptop and will you need a microphone? Will you be on a stage? Do they have a lectern, a screen and a projector if you need them? If you are speaking in a marquee at a wedding or a fundraiser, your voice can be drowned out by wind and rain, so a mic is essential. Get the answers well beforehand and you will begin to feel confident and thus able to look forward to the event.

Is there a fee?

A fee should always be determined as early as possible, especially if you are speaking at a charity event. Are you going to charge them or give your fee to the charity? Organisations such as the Women's Institute, Rotary Clubs or Inner Wheel usually have a standard fee and will sometimes pay travel expenses on top. If the job is a corporate one it can be tricky as you don't want to price yourself out of the job, but on the other hand you don't want to sell yourself short. It is as well to try to find out any fee range in advance.

Chapter 2

The audience

'The success of your presentation will be judged not by the knowledge you send but by what the listener receives.'

Lilly Walters

When you start writing you should never lose sight of the audience. What's in it for them? Are you going to help them save or make money? Make their lives easier or show them something new? What is the mood? If a boss is giving a speech to employees who know there are going to be redundancies in the company, their mood will be pretty sombre. Without sinking them deeper into the mire, the delivery style should take this into account – it should be sympathetic but powerful. Consequently, before you structure and deliver your talk think carefully about your audience. Here are some more questions:

- What is your connection with the people listening to you?
- Are they your colleagues, your superiors or members of your team?
- Are they your customers or your suppliers?
- Why should they care about what you are saying?

I can't stress enough the need to know whom you are talking to as every speech, presentation or talk should be written with that individual audience in mind. What do they want or need to know? You'd be surprised by how many people stand up and say what they want to say rather than what the audience needs, or wants, to hear.

Who is the audience?

Researching the audience is a fundamental part of preparation. You cannot write a talk until you know whom you are talking to. In order to define your audience as accurately as possible, answer these questions before you begin:

- How many people will be there?
- What is the age range?
- What is the proportion of men to women? What is the cultural and disability diversity?
- What job categories or positions will be there?

What size is the audience?

The number of people you are speaking to has a bearing on how you write and deliver your talk. It is more difficult to target the message if the audience comes from diverse backgrounds, age categories and/or have a variety of jobs, so you'll need to speak more generally if this is the case. If the space is very large, in order to hold a large audience, then you will need a microphone and probably to be on a stage, and you will be expected to be more of a performer than if you were addressing a board meeting in the office. There are lots of tips that will help you to ensure you have the right tools in the next chapter.

What age is the audience?

The age of the audience will give you a good steer as to content. If they are mostly young, they will want to know about the

How to engage with your audience

People will listen if you can:

- show them something new
- save them time, stress or money
- introduce a feel-good factor

future. If they are older, the past and present will probably interest them more.

What do they want to know?

What they want to know and what you want to tell your audience can be two very different things. You need to have a detailed objective. Ask yourself how your audience will benefit from what you are going to tell them. Most people will

undoubtedly want to know that prices are going down and the availability of various goods and services are going up, but if you can't tell them either of those things, you have to manage their expectations by writing the talk in a certain way.

What do they know already?

If some people in the audience know quite a lot about your subject and others don't it can lead to quite a tricky situation. If you repeat material some people already know it will turn them off. On the other hand, you can't ignore those people who don't have the information. Fortunately, there are certain phrases you can use to engage the whole audience and there is advice on how to do this in Chapter 3.

What are their jobs or positions?

The sort of jobs your audience do and where they work will help determine how you pitch your talk. If most of the people there are from the professions (accountants, lawyers, doctors etc) then the examples and anecdotes will need to be different from the ones you might use when speaking to a group of plumbers, electricians, farmers or builders. The structure of talks for small business owners will need to be different from those for CEOs and employees of large businesses and organisations. But whomever you are talking to, never forget that you are telling a story!

Audience breakdown

Knowing the breakdown of your audience is vital before writing the speech. People think in different ways and react differently to key words and phrases. The pictures you paint will be different, too. When speaking to a mainly female audience you will need to demonstrate empathy and

understanding to achieve successful communication rather than a more straightforward approach directed to a predominantly male audience. The choice of 'I' or 'we' can have a significant effect on how a message is received. For example:

- **Female** – 'In my opinion, we should do x, y and z, and if we do, the outcome will be...'
- **Male** – 'In my opinion, you should do x, y and z, and if you do, the outcome will be...'

The phrases are almost the same, but they transmit subtly different messages. As another example, take the situation of having to tell a sales meeting that late appointments are losing business for the company. The approaches may be as follows:

- **Female** – 'I have been wanting to talk to you about H Charles Ltd. It seems we have been late with the last three deliveries, and they are not very happy. It would be a pity to spoil such a good relationship, wouldn't it? So, I'm sure it won't happen again.'

- **Male** – 'Top of the agenda is H Charles Ltd. It seems the last three deliveries have been late, and they are not happy. We cannot afford to ruin good customer relations, so let's make sure it doesn't happen again.'

Men usually tend to be more down-to-earth and want to get to the bottom line quicker, whereas women are subtler in how they convey the message. The lesson here is to be aware of how different people consume information. The jokes you might tell should also be different depending on the breakdown of the audience.

Who are the key people in the audience?

These decision-makers should be in your mind when you're writing the talk. What will hit their buttons or tick their boxes? Do as much research as you can to get into their heads. If you want to impress the chairperson of a particular organisation and he or she is a keen football fan, why not use a footballing analogy to make a point? The inclusion of relevant anecdotes can also help to build empathy.

Chapter 3

Creation

'If you can't write your message in a sentence, you can't say it in an hour.'
Dianna Booher

Before you give a talk, you need to write it out. In order to do this, it is a very good idea to refine your message to one sentence and expand it from there. In other words, create a focusing statement, then brainstorm all the things you need to cover. I usually suggest writing these up to script the talk in full in the first instance as it helps you to get your information and thoughts in some sort of order. Reading what you have written will also help you to decide what is relevant to the story and will probably prompt you to add more.

Having researched and written the first draft, it is then a good idea to let it simmer for a while. It is amazing how much the subconscious mind can help if you give it time, so leave it for a few hours or overnight and you will probably come back to the speech with some new ideas.

Write the talk to be said, not read!

There is a big difference between writing something to be read and something to be said. When we speak to people we use language that is conversational and easily understood. If your talk is delivered in this conversational style it will go down much better with an audience. That said, although it's important not to sound as though you have swallowed a dictionary, do aim to make your talks as interesting as possible by using a variety of descriptive words. When you have written the first draft read it out loud and ask yourself if it would sound natural if you were talking to friends in the pub or at a party.

Opening remarks and introduction

It is often said that if you can't remember the introduction to a talk then it's too long. The introduction is the first step down the main road of your presentation so it needs to be arresting. There are several ways you can do this. For instance, a quotation or a fascinating fact is a good way of getting people's attention, or, as described earlier, you could bring on an interesting prop. Another good technique is to 'book end' your talk – by which I mean starting and finishing the speech with the same phrase or motif. The book end is a useful device because the audience is likely to remember the first and last things you say. This doesn't just apply to speeches, either. The British conductor Sir Thomas Beecham proclaimed there are two golden rules for an orchestra: 'Start together and finish together – the public doesn't give a damn what happens in between.' There is also a similar saying in the theatre: 'Make a good entrance and a good exit and the audience won't remember too much about the middle.'

When it comes to talks, anecdotes and quotations are often the hooks that are used to snag the audience's attention, and there are countless examples online that you can look up. You can also use case studies and actual examples to illustrate your message. Truth is often stranger than fiction and adds authenticity to your message. In his book *Speak so Your Audience will Listen* actor and author Robin Kermode cites one such attention-grabbing opening: 'In the 17th and 18th century, men shaved their heads and wore large ostentatious wigs. And when they fought duels, as they often did, they would try to flick their opponent's wig with the point of their sword and literally pull the wool over their eyes. Now I don't want to pull the wool over your eyes tonight, but I would like to tell you about...'.

Starting your talk in the middle of a story also fires the audience's curiosity, as does speaking in the present tense about past events. For example: 'It was a warm, sunny afternoon and I was walking through a wood full of bluebells, when I looked up and saw the man I would marry' instead of 'I first met the man I would marry on a warm, sunny afternoon when I was walking through a wood.' Called the 'historic present' or 'narrative present', this rhetorical device is used to create immediacy and intimacy – both of which will engage your audience and draw them into your narrative.

Key words and key points

Your key words should be persuasive and compelling, while key points should back up the title and add to it. Having introduced your topic, you need to make your first point. For a reasonably short talk, three points or subjects are usually enough. Having made a key point, make sure you have adequate detail to prove it and then construct a brief but logical link to the second key point, and then the third, etc. The aim is to lead your audience smoothly down the path until you reach your conclusion. Offer your audience something that they need or want to know and try to put yourself between your audience and possible problems. When considering what your key points should be, remember

that the greatest incentives for anyone to listen to you are:

- fear
- benefit
- relevance

A key point using the incentive of **fear** might be: 'If we don't refurbish the gym, we are going to lose members so, although we are going to have to invest a hefty sum this year, we will ensure the security of the Club going forward.' Key words here are 'refurbish', 'lose', 'invest' and 'security'.

Now, using the incentive of **benefit** you might say: 'This new robot mower may be expensive but the savings made in the cost of man hours will mean that it will have paid for itself by next year.' Key words here are 'expensive', 'savings' and 'paid'.

In terms of **relevance** you could say: 'As you may have seen on social media, more people are getting takeaways rather than cooking at home, so it is a good time to think about upgrading our takeaway menu.' Key words here are 'social media', 'takeaways', 'upgrading' and 'menu'.

So, you can see that by tapping into one of these three incentives and then carefully using key words to make your point, you engage the audience, provide concise, relevant facts and at the same time offer a solution to or at least invite engagement with the issue you are highlighting.

Visual language

The Chinese say a picture paints a thousand words and they are right, especially where speeches are concerned. If you are not using visual aids then the pictures are painted by the words you use.

For instance, instead of saying that something weighs 35kg, try using the simile 'as heavy as a large suitcase'. This immediately helps the listener to visualise what you are trying to say.

Robin Kermode again: 'In the 1960s a company selling lawn seed ran this advertising campaign: "THE BEST LAWN SEED IN THE WORLD". Their sales didn't go up when the commercial was running. Something was wrong. They soon realised that the audience didn't want the best lawn seed. What the audience wanted was the best *lawn*. So they changed their strapline to: "FOR THE BEST LAWNS IN THE WORLD". Their sales shot up.' Think about the audience, their aims and the pictures they want or need to see.

RHETORICAL TRICKS OF THE TRADE

As Chris Anderson mentioned in his TED talk, rhetoric is a way of using language to convey a spoken message more effectively, lending it greater power and making it more memorable. It is a huge subject area that we cannot possibly go into in too much depth here, so I've simply chosen a few common tricks that you can easily apply to your own writing, many of which I've used almost unconsciously when writing this book!

TRICOLONIC STRUCTURES

Also know as 'the rule of three', tricolonic mottos, slogans or catchphrases are simply groupings of three words used to express one idea more forcefully. Once you know about them, you see them everywhere, most prominently in advertising and catchphrases – 'Beanz Meanz Heinz' or 'Stop, look and listen' – but also in political speeches (Churchill's 'blood, sweat and tears'), law ('tell us the truth, the whole truth and nothing but the truth'), comedy ('an Englishman, an Irishman and a Scotsman') and many other forms of literature. You can easily incorporate some into your own writing to grab and retain listeners' attention and make the core message of your talk more memorable.

ALLITERATION

Alliteration is the repetition of the same initial sound for several words. An apt example of an appropriate alliterative phrase for this book could be the sentence: 'Proper planning and practice prevent poor performance'.

SIMILES AND METAPHORS

As already mentioned, you should aim to paint a picture with your words when you give a speech, drawing in your audience and taking them on a journey that retains their attention for the duration. Using similes and metaphors to make comparisons is a great way to do this. Many people, however, are unsure about the difference between the two (though for our purposes it doesn't actually matter whether you know which type you are using so long as it helps to create a vivid image) so here's a brief explanation that should provide some clarity:

- A simile usually includes the word 'like' or 'as' and compares two things to each other, e.g. 'as big as an elephant'.
- A metaphor simply states the comparison, e.g. 'The world is a stage'.

ANAPHORA

In rhetorical terms, anaphora is the repetition of a word or phrase at the start of successive clauses. One of the most famous examples comes from that master orator Sir Winston Churchill talking about war: 'we shall fight on the beaches, we shall fight on the landing grounds, we shall fight in the fields and in the streets, we shall fight in the hills'.

CHIASMUS

This term simply describes two successive clauses or sentences in which the key words or phrases are repeated, but in reverse order. A common, very memorable, example is: 'When the going gets tough, the tough get going'. (Technically, linguists would say this is an example of antimetabole, but for general usage it can be called chiasmus since this is the more common term.)

PUNS AND WORDPLAY

Although you should be careful about using too many jokes, especially in more formal settings, there's no doubt that humour can play a part in engaging the audience when you give a talk. Puns – the exploitation of multiple meanings of a word or of similar-sounding words – are an easy way to do this. Note that homophonic (words that sound the same but have different meanings) puns work better than homographic (words that are spelled the same but have different meanings) ones when you are speaking, since the latter rely on you seeing the word written down in order to work.

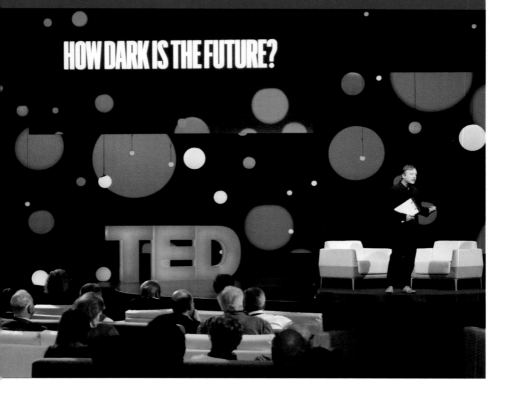

The conclusion

This is a very important part of the talk as it is what the audience will remember most. You need to summarise the major points, showing that your objectives have been met. It sounds obvious, but you should also make sure the audience knows when you have finished. Avoid prematurely saying 'and finally' or 'to summarise' – reserve those phrases until the very end – or else the audience will have switched off long before you have actually reached the end.

One useful way of concluding is to link back to the introduction (book ending, see page 27). For example:

'I said at the start that time is the one thing we have on our side, so let us make the most of it. Thank you.'

Don't end with an apology or on a negative note, such as 'I don't think I have anything left to say'. The conclusion should end on a positive: 'To conclude, despite a difficult year we now have enough money in the kitty to refurbish the village hall, and I suggest we do so without further delay.'

Tricks of the trade

USEFUL PHRASES

These are helpful phrases when you are not sure how much the audience knows about your topic:

- 'For those of us who aren't quite sure…'
- 'As I am sure you all know…'
- 'Although we are all aware of … I think some points need re-emphasising…'
- 'Many of you will be familiar with what I am about to say, but I think it bears repeating…'
- 'We all know that…'

JOKES AND ANECDOTES

If you are good at telling jokes it is great to include some but be sure they are suitable for that particular audience. Nobody expects you to be a stand-up comic; a joke that falls flat is far worse than no joke at all. The journalistic golden rule says: 'If in doubt – leave it out.' This also goes for any information you're not sure about.

QUOTATIONS

Quotations are often a good way to start a talk, or to use as your book ends. Here are a few generic quotes to give you a few ideas:

- 'May you live for as long as you like and have all you like for as long as you live.' *Unknown*. (This is an example of chiasmus – the reversal of words in successive clauses.)
- 'My father gave me these hints on speech making: be sincere, be brief, be seated.' *James Roosevelt*. (This is an example of both anaphora – the repetition of 'be' – and a tricolonic structure.)
- 'I often quote myself; it adds spice to my conversation.' *George Bernard Shaw*. (This is an example of a metaphor. It is also an example of the correct use of a semicolon.)

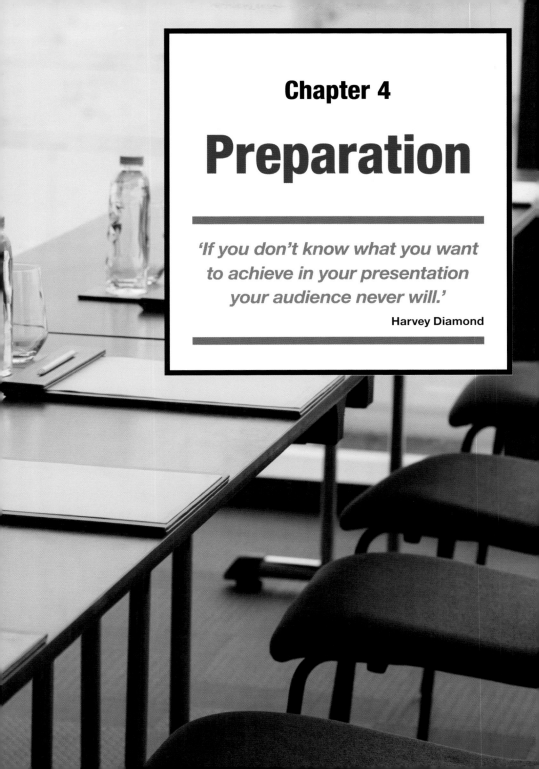

Chapter 4

Preparation

'If you don't know what you want to achieve in your presentation your audience never will.'

Harvey Diamond

The Three P's

Good speakers are made, not born (although it may help to be born with an outgoing personality), but what makes a good speaker? The answer: preparation. This applies to 1) the creation stage: writing a story with a beginning, a middle and an end; and 2) the practising stage: knowing your talk, your voice and your body. Mastering all of these will enable you to speak with confidence and conviction.

One of the things you might worry about when you get up to speak is that you'll forget everything you ever knew, including your own name. However, with proper preparation you will not only remember everything you want to say (and your name) but you will ensure you deliver all the information the audience needs in a straightforward, uncomplicated and entertaining way.

Prepare, **practise**, **perfect**. I cannot stress enough the need to prepare thoroughly, practise repeatedly and perfect your performance. If you don't, you'll be more likely to succumb to nerves, as I discovered when I did a TEDx Talk at the University of Chester in 2019, at which I think I was more nervous than I'd been for any other talk I have given. The fact that we only had 12 minutes and it was being recorded to go on to the net later meant that I had to be very disciplined and very well rehearsed. Although I'd spent time preparing the speech, unfortunately I was

unable to do a 'walk through' the day before because I was working, which meant I didn't see the stage or the equipment beforehand and, worse still, I was first on so I couldn't even see how everything worked! In this instance the situation was unavoidable, but it highlights the fact that you should always try to see the venue beforehand if at all possible as it will give you much more confidence.

Write, read, record

1 **Write** the talk out in full to get the full gist of what you want to say.

2 After you have written the talk, **read** it through to iron out any glaring grammatical errors, ensure ease of understanding and resolve any areas of uncertainty. The next step is to read it out loud so that you get an idea of how it sounds and a sense of timing. You will probably alter the first draft after you have read it a few times. Then read it to family or friends to get their views. You should aim to read it aloud 12 times if possible.

3 **Record** yourself and listen carefully. It is a painful process because the voice we hear in our heads is often quite different from the one everybody else hears but believe me, it is the best way to improve, hone and refine your talk. This is the way you get over nerves; if you are sure of what you are going to say and how you are going to say it, you will be able to enjoy standing up and delivering your talk.

Scripted talks

If you are going to read your talk then it is a good idea to underline key words. I used to do this on my script when reading the news (we always had the bulletin on paper in

> ### Be the best 'you'
>
> Although you will see lots of speakers you admire, never try to imitate them. By all means learn from them but it is always best to be you. My advice is to work hard and develop your own style, which should fit you like a second skin.

case the speech prompter went down). You can mark it in any way you like, such as using different-coloured pens and symbols to help you remember to vary your tone of voice and alter the pace. It is a good idea to write bullet points in different colours, too, to make them stand out more.

How to practise effectively

Once you have prepared your talk thoroughly, check these points before you begin rehearsing:

1 Was your introduction interesting and powerful enough to seize the audience's attention? As I have said before, you need to grab people within the first two or three seconds and to do this the message must be absolutely clear in your head, otherwise you will not be able to 'perform' it properly. Rehearsal, then, is key.

2 Do you feel strongly enough about your topic to sound enthusiastic? If not, why not? You will not come across as sincere and authentic unless your enthusiasm shines through.

Once you are sure your talk will meet its objective and everything is logical and clear, with your key points set out in a logical order, linked to the one before it, you can start practising your presentation. Here are some tips:

■ First of all, decide how you are going to deliver the speech. Are you going to read from a paper script or an electronic teleprompter? Might you just use notes or are you going to memorise the whole thing? This obviously has an effect on your performance and how you practise.

■ I find one of the most painful things about public speaking is having to constantly look at and analyse your voice and your body! Nevertheless, until you feel absolutely happy with how you look and how you sound you will not come across as confident and natural. Confidence also means competence, which is essential in business presentations. Stand in front of a full-length mirror and talk to yourself. The more you do this the more normal it will become.

■ It is best to rehearse in bite-size chunks whichever way you decide to present your material. Don't overload yourself, otherwise you may begin to eat away at your confidence levels and knock your self-belief if you are not as good as you think you should be right from the start.

■ If you opt to memorise your speech, by all means use your script or notes at the start and then gradually lose them as

you feel more comfortable and know the text better.

■ If the venue is going to be a large one, get a spotlight and set it to shine in your eyes when you are rehearsing. This can be a valuable way of helping you to get used to auditorium lights and it means you won't feel uncomfortable when you step out on to a brightly lit podium or stage. Anything that makes you feel comfortable will help you come across as yourself.

■ There is an actor's trick that can help you to shed the natural inhibitions we all feel at the thought of making a fool of ourselves in front of other people. Hold your second finger and thumb together and think of something that makes you happy. This could be an event or an emotion. Concentrate really hard on visualising the memory and the feeling as you keep your fingers and thumbs pressed hard together. Do this a number of times until whenever you hold your fingers and thumbs the memory or emotion immediately comes to mind. Then, just before you are about to walk on to the stage, hold your finger and thumb together. It is amazing how this simple exercise can help you feel calm and enthusiastic about making your speech.

Tailoring your speech to the event

BUSINESS PRESENTATIONS

Business presentations, like any other type, should tell a story. I remember doing a lot of work with scientists in the soda ash plant at a large chemical company. The company wanted them to explain to the local residents what was going on at the plant. None of the scientists or technicians were keen to speak and they thought their subject was so boring that nobody would want to listen. If you were just to talk about soda ash and its components then indeed it could be a boring subject, but if you describe what it is used for it then becomes quite fascinating. Once I had helped them realise that people were interested in the fact that soda ash is used to make washing powder, glass and dyestuffs, among many other things we use every day, I got them thinking and changed their mindset. We went on to devise a presentation describing and showing greenhouses in the desert, multicoloured clothes hanging out to dry in Italy, and a beautiful infinity swimming pool with a spectacular view high in the mountains in Spain, highlighting that soda ash is also a water softener. Another firm I coached made drainpipes. Again, the engineers had no interest in talking about drains or drainpipes. However, once I'd urged them to think about the end users of their pipes, they produced a stunning presentation showing water being

Virtual presentations

If you are presenting on Zoom, Skype, or any other online platform, you need to be aware that your face is probably the only part of your body that will be on show. Again, the Three P's are important – prepare, practise and perfect. Prepare what you are going to say as if it were a speech being given to a roomful of people and practise by looking into the camera on your computer so you can see the facial expressions you use. Video yourself so you can review how you come across and check that you appear relaxed when you are speaking. Make sure that the background is clear of clutter – there should be no coffee cups or piles of papers on show.

delivered to African villages, storm drains preventing monsoon rains from ruining crops in Malaysia, and a rather quirky one of sewage pipes!

Once you've come up with your story, build in visual aids in the form of graphs, images and flow charts, all of which help to deliver what can sometimes be a complicated message in an interesting and thought-provoking way. Use everyday language as much as is feasible; 'paradigm' and 'dialectic', for instance, are not technical terms that specialists have to use, so avoid academese and bizspeak as much as possible.

Repeating the presentation

Often, the essential framework of a talk might be used again at a later date. However, given that it will be delivered to a different audience, it is essential to tailor and adapt the talk each time you reuse it in order to keep you and the message fresh. To help you adapt the talk, bear these points in mind:

- Once again, ask yourself what part your talk will play in the event, meeting or conference.
- Are there any new speakers?
- Has the objective changed?
- Think carefully about your audience: size, age, who will be present? Check that your introduction is still appropriate and change any key points to suit this group.
- Bring in a local aspect if possible.

TEAM PRESENTATIONS

If you are part of a team, rehearsing together is crucial. Although you know what each speaker is going to say, always look interested when they are speaking, however many times you have heard it before. If you look bored, your audience will pick up on this and begin to get bored too.

MEETINGS

Meetings are a fact of life in the corporate world. The aim is to get the most out of the meeting in the least amount of time, and they should be productive, informative and

motivating. Badly managed meetings waste time and can have a negative effect on company morale and affect teamwork.

Try to ensure that only the relevant people are asked to attend and that everything is organised in advance. This includes appointing a chairperson if there isn't one already in place, and then writing an agenda and circulating it. The role of the chairperson is to control the meeting. This includes ensuring the meeting starts and finishes on time; be realistic – don't try to fit in too much. The chair should also insist that questions and comments 'go through the chair' if it is a formal meeting, in order to keep the meeting disciplined and to time. If everyone starts embarking on their own agendas, chaos will reign. Make sure everybody is given equal time to air their

views and if other important topics are brought up, fix a different time to talk about them or arrange another meeting if the situation is urgent. If possible, don't introduce any extra topics as they will make everything and everybody run late. Remember – time is money and the longer people are away from their desks, the more it costs the organisation.

In terms of protocol during the meeting, absences and apologies should be given at the start of the meeting as well as any essential or urgent information. The chair should then thank everybody for attending and get the meeting underway. Again, preparation is vital if you are to now get your points across or deliver information. Write out your input beforehand and time it. You need to be succinct and to the point

Time to stand and stare

Think about the venue where you will give your speech. A meeting room on the top floor of a city skyscraper might be so familiar to the people who work there that they never think about the view, but for visitors it will be spectacular, so give them a few moments to have the opportunity to stand at the window and stare at the vista before they sit down and listen to you.

to get your message across in limited time. Ensure that you also have the correct props to hand. Whiteboards and flipcharts are more commonly used at board or informal company meetings than PowerPoint, but the latter can be shown on a computer on the table if the meeting is small and a large screen would be overpowering.

Notes or minutes should be distributed as soon as possible after the meeting.

Where should I sit during a meeting?

Where do you sit if you are chairing and speaking at a meeting? The 'power position' is at the head of the table where everyone can see you. The seat opposite the power position is usually reserved for a client or guest. If there are no seats at either end of the table, the power position is in the middle where you have the best view of those at the meeting and where they can see you.

You might decide to sit rather than stand to make your presentation, in which case the same rules apply as when standing: know your subject, make eye contact and speak clearly.

NETWORKING GROUPS

You won't be expected to give a presentation at a networking event but

you'll need to have a 30-second elevator pitch (see box) prepared so that you can tell people quickly and succinctly what you do.

Smile as you walk into the room; we make up 90 per cent of our mind about people in about three seconds. To that end, dress to impress – you want to stand out and be noticed, but remember that you are the image of your organisation.

Read body language; don't try to enter a 'closed' group as you might not get a good reception. If you are part of a group, it is polite to engage bystanders and those on their own and to introduce people to each other.

You probably won't have time to do much business on the night so arrange a meeting with a targeted person in order to discuss further business matters, and be focused about what you want to achieve. And don't forget to take plenty of business cards!

SEMINARS AND CONFERENCES

You are more than likely to be on a stage, sometimes with video screens behind you, so to look confident, competent and professional you have to be extra well prepared. If you can, try to rehearse the speech in front of an audience. You don't need a whole roomfull, but if you can hire your local village hall for an hour and drag in friends, family or colleagues it will be time well spent as it will give you a sense of size and scale.

INTERNATIONAL CONFERENCES

International conferences are much the same as national ones, except that you may be working with an interpreter if there are no subtitles running on a screen behind you.

Elevator pitches

These fast-paced pitches originally started in Hollywood, where prospective screenwriters would try to collar movie execs as they went up in a lift or elevator. They only had about 30 seconds to state their case, so they made their pitch fast and slick. It is a good idea to perfect yours so that you can roll it out when needed. Be concise when you write it and time it to make sure it is about 30 seconds long.

If this is the case, it is vital to find the right interpreter. You then need time to go through the presentation with them to make sure they understand any colloquial or technical terms. Understand that the standard of interpreter can vary enormously. When we were working in China, for instance, my colleague, William Hanson, found out the translator had been talking about the 'duck' of Edinburgh rather than the duke! Therefore, depending on the quality of the interpreter, you might find you need to change some of the words for easy interpretation. On this occasion, if we had said 'Prince Philip' rather than 'the Duke of Edinburgh', the interpreter might have understood better.

If you are speaking live it is important to give your interpreter time to translate your words. When I work in China I have to be aware that it takes a lot longer to say something in Mandarin than it does in English. If the speech is scripted, you and the interpreter will both have copies of the script, so it is a good idea to break it down into roughly two-sentence chunks and then hand over to the interpreter.

Don't forget that your audience has to listen to everything twice, so keep it short and snappy.

At the end of a conference or seminar, try to get feedback from an English speaker to make sure that what you said was interpreted correctly.

Even if no interpreter is required, your delivery when speaking at an international conference should be a bit slower than normal so that the audience can listen and read more easily.

POLITICAL SPEECHES

In this cynical day and age, the most important thing for a politician when speaking is to be sincere and not to promise what can't be delivered. Cut the waffle and be concise. Ten minutes at a local event and 20 minutes for a major rally should easily suffice. By all means read great political speeches and listen to brilliant orators but you should also learn to develop your own style and always be yourself. It is *you* they will be voting for, not a poor imitation of someone else.

Enthusiasm for what you are saying is essential whether you are making a speech or talking to constituents on the doorstep and at local surgeries. Listening skills are also important and thorough research into the hopes, aspirations and concerns of possible voters will mean your speeches will be relevant. Your audience may only have a vague idea of what goes on behind the political scenes so try to explain what can be a complicated situation as plainly as possible.

TOUR GUIDES AND GROUP LEADERS

Kim Dewdney is a qualified Blue Badge Tourist Guide in London and has these pearls of wisdom: 'Always be aware of the

What if there are several speakers?

At some events there may be more than one speaker. If that is the case, try to find out who else is speaking and what they are talking about, as discussed in Chapter 1. And I'll say it again: it really is bad manners to go way over your allotted time as you are using up the audience's concentration for the next speaker.

"Top Visual Priority" or TVP. That's the thing that everyone is going to look at so address it first – even if it is not what you want to talk about. If you don't then your audience is going to spend a lot of time not listening to you but looking at the TVP and wondering what it is and why you haven't mentioned it.' When guiding, an obvious example of this scenario may arise in Trafalgar Square in London, where you might want to speak about something small and detailed, but your party is looking towards Nelson's Column. In this case, it makes sense to talk about that particular TVP first.

HOW TO WELCOME GUESTS OR THE AUDIENCE

Depending on the formality of the occasion, you may have to mention the most important attendees or guests. Here are some examples of titles and how to address people holding different positions in a formal way:

- Ladies and Gentlemen
- My Lords, Ladies and Gentlemen
- The Royal Family: Your Majesty, Your Royal Highness
- Prime Minister: Prime Minister
- Ministers: Minister
- Presidents: Mr or Madam President
- Dukes and Duchesses: Your Grace or Duke/Duchess
- Anglican Archbishops: Archbishop
- Anglican Bishops: Bishop
- Cardinals: Your Eminence or Cardinal
- Catholic Bishops: Your Grace or My Lord Bishop
- Chief Rabbi: Rabbi
- Imam: Imam
- Ambassadors: Your Excellency or Mr/Madam Ambassador
- High Commissioners: Your Excellency or High Commissioner
- Lords and ladies: Lord or Lady and their name
- Mayors: Mr or Madam Mayor

IF YOU ARE INTRODUCING THEM:
- Her Majesty the Queen
- His/Her Royal Highness and their name
- The Right Honourable (name), MP the Prime Minister
- The Right Honourable (name), the Minister of State for…
- The President of (name of country)
- His/Her Grace The Duke or Duchess of (name of Duchy)
- The Most Reverend and Right Honourable the Lord Archbishop of (name of archdiocese)
- His Excellency, The Ambassador for (name of country)
- His Excellency, The High Commissioner for (name of country)
- Lords and ladies: Lord or Lady and their name
- Mayors: Mr or Madam Mayor of (name of city/town)

NON-PROFESSIONAL OR FAMILY GATHERINGS
Most of these gatherings don't need formal introductions, but guests should be welcomed and any particularly important guests or those who have travelled a long way should be referred to.

CHARITY EVENTS

When asked to speak about a charity at an event ensure that you know who the key people to thank are, the amount of money raised that year, and plans for the year ahead. Use any relevant stories or anecdotes and propose a toast. Sometimes, complex issues may be in the spotlight, and you may have to explain why certain decisions have been made. Do this by stating the facts as simply as you can without ever talking down to your audience.

If, however, you are the guest speaker at a charity fundraiser then you may have been asked simply to entertain the audience, in which case you can choose your subject. However, it makes sense to try to link it back in some way to the particular charity, so do your research.

AFTER-DINNER SPEECHES

Whether the talk is for business or pleasure your objective must be clear to everyone. If it isn't clear to you then it certainly won't be to your audience. An original point of view that will inspire and gives people something to think about is often what is needed, but it all depends on the occasion. Talking to the organisers and researching your audience will help you to decide on the topics that will suit both them and you. It is also important to appreciate the ambience and purpose of the event or celebration. An amusing story about yourself can help build credibility as well as building a bridge with your audience so that they feel you are one of them. That said, although you are there to entertain the audience, after-dinner speeches shouldn't be a series of unrelated jokes and don't always have to be light-hearted. If you do choose to tell

> ## Include everyone
>
> Make sure the stories you tell are not too embarrassing and try not to include too many 'in' jokes that may exclude some sections of the audience.

jokes, link them together so they become an integral part of the story.

For less formal events, getting people to interact is a good way to engage them. Ask for answers to a question or play a simple game as an ice-breaker, such as 'Heads and Tails'. All you need is a two-sided coin. As you flip it, ask people to put their hands on their head or their tail. Those who get it wrong have to sit down . The winner is the one left standing at the end.

RETIREMENT

When people retire there is usually a wealth of stories based in the workplace that you can draw upon. If you know the person well you might be asked to recount their life in the company, how they worked their way up and then thank them for everything they have done for the organisation over the years before proposing a toast to their future.

Today, however, people tend to work for more than one company or for themselves, and often retire earlier. If this is the case, the retirement party might be more of a family-based celebration, in which case it is more appropriate to talk about their hobbies and plans for the retirement rather than work done in the past.

WEDDINGS

Speeches at weddings range from being truly entertaining to absolutely dire. It is a

great honour to be asked to speak at one since it is one of the most important days in the bride and groom's life. The speech is not a licence to talk for as long as you want, though. Remember, people are there to enjoy the whole occasion and, depending on when the speeches take place, will likely want to get on with the meal or to hit the dance floor.

There are numerous books and websites that provide sample speeches that can act as a template for you to personalise, and these are a good place to start. Even if you don't use these, preparation needs to be taken seriously, as does rehearsing the speech, especially if it is going to be on video or in the Cloud for perpetuity. If video or a slideshow is to be used, check the technology beforehand so that everything runs as smoothly as possible.

The father or proposer of the bride

The father, mother or proposer of the bride needs to do several things in their speech:

- Welcome the groom's family and friends.
- Say nice things about the bride.
- Relate suitable anecdotes and stories about when the bride was little.
- Propose a toast to the health and happiness of the bride and groom.

The bridegroom

In response, the bridegroom should thank the father or proposer of the bride's toast. In addition, he should:

- Respond to any worldly wisdom given by the bride's father.
- Say how happy he is to be joining the bride's family.
- Tell an amusing story about how they met.
- Thank his parents or guardians.
- Thank the guests for coming and for their gifts.
- Say thanks to the best man, ushers and any helpers.
- Say a big thank you to the bridesmaids and give them their gifts.
- Raise a toast to the bridesmaids.

The bride

More brides give speeches these days, and she should:

- Say thanks to her new husband.
- Thank the attendants.
- Thank her parents or guardians for everything they have done for her.

The best man

The best man's speech is usually the one people look forward to hearing the most. He should:

- Compliment the bridesmaids.
- Tell stories about the groom. However, these should not embarrass him, or the bride, or any relatives. There should also be no offensive jokes.

FUNERALS

There are many reasons why you might be asked to deliver a eulogy at a funeral: perhaps you are a good friend of the family; perhaps you are a good communicator; perhaps you're both. Whatever the reason, collaboration with the family of the deceased is vital. Jo Wheeler is a celebrant and has this to say: 'It is so important to speak to as many

Readings for weddings and funerals

Finding the right passages can be tricky and takes time. Here are examples of two short pieces, the first for a wedding and the second for a funeral.

A NATIVE AMERICAN WEDDING POEM
'Now you will feel no rain,
For each of you will be shelter to the other.
Now you will feel no cold,
For each of you will be warmth to the other.
Now there is no more loneliness,
For each of you will be companion to the other.
Now you are two bodies,
But there is one life before you.
Go now to your dwelling place,
To enter into the days of your togetherness.
And may your days be good and long upon the earth.'

Unknown

SOMETHING BEAUTIFUL REMAINS
'The tide recedes but leaves behind bright seashells on the sand.
The sun goes down, but gentle warmth still lingers on the land.
The music stops, and yet it echoes on in sweet refrains...
For every joy that passes, something beautiful remains.'

Unknown

people as you can, collect memories and recollections; impressions and idiosyncrasies. For instance, a seemingly outgoing and gregarious individual might also be a deeply private and quiet person within the home. A grumpy and officious boss might spend his spare time serving in soup kitchens.' Looking at photos can help jog memories and bring snippets of information to mind.

On the day itself, your delivery of your speech will likely be affected by your closeness to the deceased, the location and the environment. If you are speaking in a church then the words you use and the way you express yourself will be different from if you are speaking at a green burial site in a field.

In many cases the local vicar or priest will take the service and deliver the eulogy but again, close collaboration is needed to make the address sound personal. Jo Wheeler again: 'Too many eulogy writers fall back on the safety of a "life timeline", but how about considering the year of their birth? What was going on? What was happening in their part of the world at that time? Think about how their lifestyle changed from their upbringing to that of their own offspring, if they had any.'

GRADUATION CEREMONIES

It is a very important day when someone graduates after a long time spent studying, so if you are asked to say a few words make sure you are absolutely up to speed with the subjects they have graduated in. If you have known them a long time, your son or daughter for example, some non-embarrassing childhood stories can be included. If it is an older person then interesting anecdotes about their life before taking up their studies will fit the bill.

Celebrant for a day

I have personal experience of giving eulogy, although being a celebrant for a day wasn't something I was expecting! My turn came when a very good friend asked me to conduct the funeral for her father at their local crematorium. I had written addresses and eulogies in the past but never actually conducted a service. I did my research and was told that the service should last no longer than 30 minutes. This didn't give a lot of time for the actual service by the time everybody had got in and out, so I needed to find out how many family members were speaking or reading and plan my eulogy accordingly. Because I didn't actually know my friend's father, I spent a lot of time talking to the family and getting to know him. I was quite alarmed when I was told I had to lead the procession and then to be aware of the 'traffic lights' in the lectern. These go from green to red to help make sure you finish on time. Everything went well thanks to my preparation, and it was an experience I will never forget.

IMPORTANT BIRTHDAYS

Big birthdays are usually an excuse for a party and a speech to go with it. This type of speech is similar to wedding speeches. There are always lots of stories that can be told about the birthday boy or girl and they can be amusing, even apocryphal, but not unkind. If you are suddenly asked to 'say a few words' then the mantra 'past, present and future' can come to your aid. You can talk about their younger days, where they are now and take a guess at the future, depending on their age.

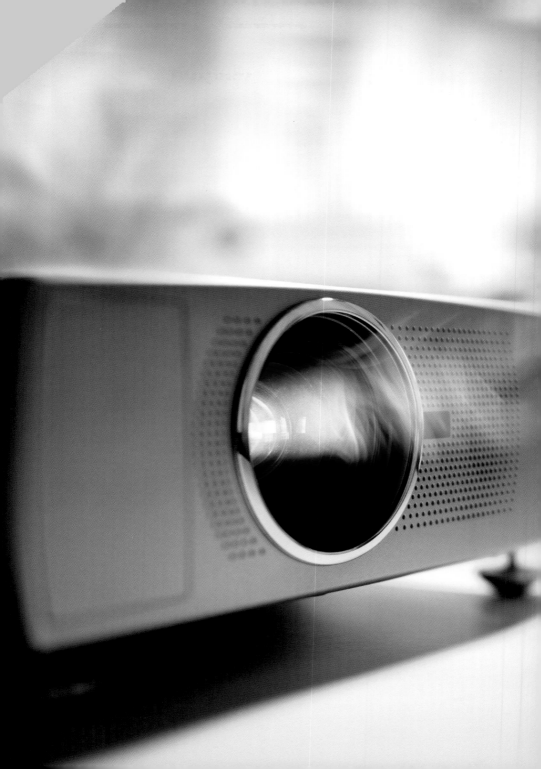

Chapter 5

Visual aids and how to use them effectively

*'Create your own visual style ...
let it be unique for yourself and
yet identifiable for others.'*

Orson Welles

In this chapter I am going to talk about aids for professional and business presentations only; I will cover visuals for weddings, parties and other events in Chapter 6. Visual aids are there to help the audience understand and enjoy your talk, not to help you remember your speech. Used well, they will enhance your talk; used badly, they can confuse the message. In order to prepare clear visual aids it is critical that you are clear what your message is.

There are many different types of visual aids available to us today – photographs, cartoons, illustrations, animation, video and audio as well as more traditional graphs, infographics and data simulations. Any or all of these can help to make your talk more interesting – as long as they are used effectively. It is as well to remember that too many slides can take some of the attention away from the speaker and on to the screen and in some instances having no slides at all can sometimes be better than having a load of mediocre ones. That said, most talks benefit from good visuals and for some they can mean the difference between success and failure.

Traditional visuals

Traditional visual aids are text slides, photos, illustrations, graphs and pie charts.

- Text slides should emphasise the structure of a talk and lead the audience through the points you wish to cover.
- Good photos help to add interest and colour to a presentation, and illustrations should tell a story without the speaker having to give complicated information.
- Graphs and pie charts are a useful but not particularly thrilling means to

enhance your presentation, so be innovative and look for more exciting ways to tell your story.

- Infographics, for instance, can help present complicated information quickly and clearly by using graphics to enhance our grasp of patterns and trends.
- The same principles apply to whiteboards and flipcharts. Keep the words and bullet points uncluttered and simple so we can easily spot trends and retain the information.

PowerPoint, Keynote and Prezi

There are three main presentation tools in business: PowerPoint, Keynote (for Mac), and Prezi. PowerPoint is universal, but some people find Keynote preferable to use because it has really good typography and graphics. Prezi is an alternative to these; instead of comprising a linear succession of slides, it is two-dimensional, which means you can zoom in and out to focus on what you want to.

Like all visual aids, these are all brilliant tools provided that they are used properly. Beware, however, that PowerPoint slides with a headline followed by multiple bullet points or long phrases are the surest way to lose an audience's attention. Many presenters are now aware of the problem of this phenomenon, dubbed 'death by PowerPoint', and have responded by reducing the number of slides they use and instead cramming loads of data on to just a few. I am afraid this is not the answer because it can also erode audience concentration; a complex slide might take a couple of minutes or more to explain. It is much more effective to divide the information on to three or four simpler slides that you can click through in the same amount of time.

WHAT MAKES A GOOD SLIDE?

There is really only one secret to good slides and that is simplicity. Each slide should be used to make one point only. Slides that contain too much information, or too many illustrations, look cluttered and are difficult to follow. Too many words make the text small and difficult to read. As a general guideline, it is best to have only six lines of text per slide and six words per line.

Graphs and diagrams should be similarly uncluttered. If you feel that it is really important for your audience to have information in the form of complicated tables or diagrams, it is better to give them a hard copy at the end of your presentation.

David McCandless is an expert at turning data into understanding with the use of innovative slides. At TED Global in 2010 he showed two slides. The first was titled 'Who has the Biggest Military Budget?' and showed ten squares of different sizes, each representing a country in proportion to the size of their military budgets. The USA's square was by far the largest. The second slide showed squares representing military budgets as a percentage of GDP. Here, the USA slipped to eighth place, behind Myanmar, Jordan, Georgia and Saudi Arabia. In just two slides the viewpoint was dramatically changed. That's what I call a good slide!

TED's Tom Reilly also speaks about the need to manage cognitive load when creating your presentation: 'With a talk and slides you have two streams of cognitive output running in parallel. The speaker

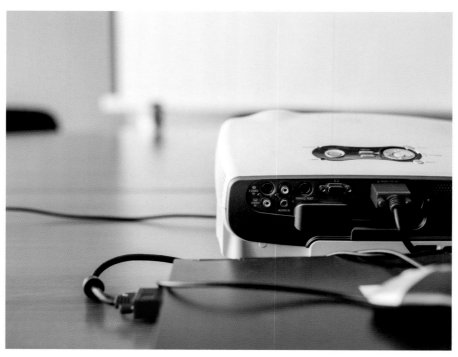

needs to blend both streams into a master mix. A complicated slide with lots of components means the audience member's brain has to decide whether to focus on your words, your slides, or both.' This can be quite tiring for them. If you make your presentation as easy as possible to absorb then you have a much better chance of keeping your audience with you.

HOW TO USE SLIDES

To me, the biggest crime when presenting is to read verbatim what is written on the slide. How many times have you seen people talking to the screen, sometimes completely turning their backs on the group they are addressing?! I cannot stress enough that there is no point in repeating on the slide what you are saying on stage. The audience will read ahead so by the time you cover a specific point they

will have moved on. It is also rather insulting and shows a lack of preparation and respect for those listening. As I said at the start of this chapter, visual aids are there to help the audience understand and enjoy your talk, not to help you remember it.

When you are showing the slides, use builds and colours to differentiate distinctive elements of information and add words and images through a series of clicks to focus people's attention on one point at a time. Make your slides as interesting and creative as possible without being distracting. If your work is visual, focus on the visuals. For a short visual presentation, you could use up to 100 images with some slides shown for only a couple of seconds. The use of silence can be very powerful here; you don't need to talk about each one – let the visuals explain themselves.

Do a dry run, or three

We often get too close to a subject when we are very familiar with it, so try testing your presentation, especially your slides, on family or friends. Ask them what they understood and what they didn't. Look critically at the technical side. Are the slides sharp and bright? Do the videos play OK? Are the transitions slick enough? Are the fonts the right ones? If there are any technical glitches, running through your talk a number of times will help you sort things out well in advance.

For an average presentation of 40–45 minutes it is most effective to show approximately one slide every two minutes. However, this does not mean you have to use 20 slides – you could use fewer. Bear in mind, though, that during the speech it is important not to leave slides on screen once you've finished talking about them. Go to a blank, black slide or one bearing your company logo. This means the audience can have a bit of a break from images and pay more attention to your words. They will also be ready to soak up more images when they reappear.

Make it personal

Try to personalise your slides as much as possible. If you use the standard software it can be hard to differentiate them. If you're showing a lot of photos use black as the background as it will make them stand out but, if possible, for maximum impact photographs should be shown 'full bleed', which in printing terms means it should cover the whole screen. Always use pictures with the highest resolution

possible to avoid any pixilation when they are projected on large screens.

It's usually best to employ one typeface for your presentation but don't use excessively thin fonts and too many italics as they are hard to read, especially on a dark background; bold typefaces are best. Use 24 points or larger and at the most only three sizes per presentation: a large size for titles and headlines, a medium size for your main concepts and a small size for your secondary ideas. If you're going to put type over a photo, make sure you position it where your audience can read it. When looking at font colours, black on white – a dark colour on a white background – or yellow or white on black are good because they stand out and are easy to read. When you have prepared your presentation, look at it on your computer or your TV. Ask yourself: Is it easy to read? Are the images clear?

Cover all your bases before the big day

Even if you send your presentation in advance, it is always advisable to take a

USB stick with you. Before sending the presentation over the internet or copying it to USB, put all the files into a folder and compress the folder into a ZIP file. If you are using several video clips make sure you label each clip clearly. It is usually safer to take your own laptop, but make sure it's compatible with the projector at the venue and take a variety of leads and adapters along.

It is also very important to research any licences and overcome any copyright issues. This includes images, photos, music, video and particular fonts. If you don't, you could end up spending hundreds of pounds in royalties and rights.

You may also have to give credits to photographers, composers and music and photo libraries.

Time spent researching and resolving these issues and liaising with the client to check out the equipment and software will ensure that your presentation goes as smoothly as possible and that your message is heard.

Transitions

Transitions during a slide show are many and varied but beware that they can take the audience's focus away from the main story. 'Shimmer', 'sparkle', 'confetti', 'twirl' and 'clothesline' are all Keynote transitions,

but they can be a bit gimmicky. Cuts and dissolves are usually best. Although it's not cast in stone, when using a cut, you're moving to a new idea, whereas with a dissolve the two slides should be linked in some way. You can use cuts and dissolves in the same presentation but if there is no reason for a transition, don't use one just for the sake of it. You may think it makes your presentation look more dynamic and up-to-date, but if it ends up confusing your audience then you will have defeated its purpose.

Whiteboards

Whiteboards are extremely useful tools for presenters as they can be interactive, allowing people to contribute to a presentation from different sites. This can be in the form of handwriting or graphics. To use them well, however, takes a bit of practice if you want your presentation to look smooth and seamless. It is worth spending some time rehearsing to ensure your handwriting looks professional and is easily legible. It sounds an obvious point, but if people are having difficulty deciphering your text then they are probably not giving their full attention to what you are saying.

As for slides, use different colours to make different points and don't cram the screen with too much information. Try to stand to one side of the board when you are writing so people get more than just your back view, and when you are speaking always turn to face the audience.

Flipcharts

Flipcharts are widely used when making presentations in small venues, such as meeting rooms and offices, and the same rules as for whiteboards apply. It is better to use several pages than to put too many

points on one sheet, which will likely make the message look messy and confusing.

Video

Video can really enhance a presentation, but the footage must be well shot, well lit and with good sound quality. It is usually worth spending some money to get your video shot and edited professionally. After all, you are the professional, the expert in your field, so make sure all elements of your presentation are as professional as you are. However, it is worth saying that you should only use video to enhance your story – don't be tempted to use it as a filler. Depending on the length of your presentation, you could use three or four clips, but don't make them too long. People have come to listen to you, not to go to the movies.

Audio

Good crisp sound is crucial when making any sort of speech or presentation. Whether it's the microphone you are using or the music you are playing, it must be played at the right volume and be clear. This can be quite a challenge if the sound system in the venue isn't up to scratch. Again, it is essential to do some advance research. Try to speak to a technician and find out what sound system they use, the power of the amplifier and the number and size of the speakers. If you can't get to the venue beforehand, this information will give you some idea about the potential sound quality.

If the mic is hand-held, try to have a quick rehearsal to see how close you need to hold it. If that is not possible, watch the other speakers and learn from them. If the mic is fixed, either on a lectern or your lapel, remember not to swing your head

about too much. Try to keep your mouth in line with the mic or you could end up sounding like a badly tuned radio. If you like to move around when giving a talk, ask for a radio mic. This will have a battery pack that attaches to a belt or waistband, which is something to remember if you happen to be wearing a dress.

Handouts

It is best not to provide any handouts until after you have finished your speech or presentation. If your audience has them ahead of time they will have read what you are going to say and will almost certainly switch off. If your information is quite complicated then before you start tell everyone that they will receive notes or handouts after the presentation before they leave. It goes without saying that any literature should be well constructed and of the highest quality.

Chapter 6

Using your voice and body

'Be still when you have nothing to say, when genuine passion moves you, say what you've got to say, and say it hot.'

DH Lawrence

Let's start with the voice. What is a good voice, how do you say it 'hot'? The voice is like an instrument, which when properly played will enable you to connect with and beguile your audience. A rich, melodious voice can be very persuasive and very powerful when used effectively and is a great advantage to any speaker. William Gladstone, who possessed a deep, musical voice, said: 'Ninety men in every hundred in the crowded professions will probably never rise above mediocrity because the training of the voice is entirely neglected and considered of no importance.'

Sadly, though, most people have no idea how they sound since very few of us bother to listen to our voices. This is a shame, because whether you are chatting with friends at home, colleagues at work, giving a talk or making a speech, the way you use your voice is vital. This is true in most situations, contrary to popular opinion. People sometimes say that they're not really giving a talk, they're just giving their team an update, but the word 'just' here reveals a lack of passion and clarity. If the speaker is bored by the subject, then so will the audience be. You should never 'just' give information.

How to speak clearly

So, how can you inject passion and clarity into your speaking? Start by speaking slightly slower and lower than normal; nerves tend to make us speed up or use the voice's higher register. Projection and articulation are also key: open your mouth! Many people mumble and don't open their mouths wide enough to articulate the words. If you don't open your mouth, the audience can't hear you. Recording your voice will help you know when you are speaking clearly, and you can also try these simple exercises:

1 Stick your tongue out as far as you can and then count from one to 20. This will open the throat and make your speech clearer. At drama school we were also taught to say a nursery rhyme with the tongue sticking out. I alternate between the two.

2 Make a 'trilling' sound with the tongue. Place it near the front of the mouth behind your teeth and 'trill' a tune. Preferably, do this when you are alone – I generally trill my favourite tunes in the car.

3 Say 'brrr' in a way that makes your lips vibrate. This is great for getting blood to flow to the lips.

TONGUE TWISTERS

Below is a set of trusted tongue twisters that I use whenever I am teaching voice production in order to increase the agility of the tongue, lips and mouth. Repeat each line three times, beginning with a whisper and increasing the volume through the second and third repeats. Try to keep the words clear and sharp and take care to pronounce the 't's' and 'd's' at the end of words.

- Twist the twine tightly round the tree trunks.
- Did Dora dare to deceive David deliberately?
- Kate Cooney carefully closed the kitchen cupboards.
- Gregory Gartside gained good grades in Greek grammar.
- Naughty Nora has no nice neighbours.
- Little Larry Lester lolled lazily on the lilo.
- Peggy Babcock, Babcock Peggy.
- Red leather, yellow leather, red lorry, yellow lorry.
- Unique New York, New York unique.
- Fresh fried fish.
- A cracked cricket critic.
- Try tying the twine round the tree twigs.
- She sells seashells on the seashore, the shells that she sells are seashells I'm sure.

All these exercises work on different levels. They open the voice and limber up all the muscles we use for enunciation. They will enable you to achieve clear, concise speech if practised regularly.

BREATHING FOR SPEECH

These tips will help you to control and use your breath properly:

1 Breathe in and say the months of the year as you expel the breath.
2 Try humming and filling the resonators in your head so that you can feel the head throbbing.
3 Practise saying words in an exaggerated way so that you can feel the tongue, lips and mouth moving.
4 Now try using these two phrases while raising and lowering the voice; take a deep breath before each sentence:
    'I can make my voice rise higher and higher and higher.'
    'I can make my voice go lower and lower and lower.'

VOCAL EXERCISES – *Expression*

If a voice has no expression no one will listen to it, no matter how important the message. So, it is vital that you learn to use your vocal range to its full advantage. Try saying the phrases below as directed to see how expression can affect delivery:

Say aloud:	'That was a good film.'
With more feeling:	'That was a great film.'
Aim the pitch at the top:	'That was a brilliant film.'
Normal:	'That was a good film.'
Down:	'That was an average film.'
Right down:	'That was a terrible film.'

Another useful exercise is to read out a section of a newspaper or magazine and record yourself. Adapt your delivery as if:

you are speaking at a wedding
you are speaking at a funeral
you are addressing a large crowd
you are talking to a group of children

The same text should sound completely different each time you read it, proving that it is not just what you say that is important, but the way that you say it.

Now try reading this sentence, stressing each word in bold:

'**Did** you eat my chocolates?'
'Did **you** eat my chocolates?'
'Did you **eat** my chocolates?'
'Did you eat **my** chocolates?'
'Did you eat my **chocolates**?'

The emphasis changes the meaning of each sentence, so when you are writing a speech be aware of which words you need to stress to deliver a clear message.

Read and record the lines again, this time as if you are slightly amused, then as if you

are angry, and hear the difference. If you have young children record the stories you read to them, especially the ones in which there are a number of different characters, so that you can try out using the whole of your vocal range. Doing so also helps to get rid of hang-ups or shyness.

Alternatively/additionally, read this children's rhyme in three different ways and record the different versions:

Five important P's

- **Pace** – variations of speed.
- **Pitch** – not too high or low. Feel comfortable.
- **Phrasing** – think about what you are saying. Emphasise stress points.
- **Pause** – very important – this gives your audience a chance to absorb what you are saying.
- **Projection** – not shouting. Produce your voice with plenty of controlled breathing.

> ## *'The most precious things in speech are the pauses.'*
> **Sir Ralph Richardson**

'Minding Manners'
'Feeling angry, feeling mad
Try not to make others sad
There's no excuse for being rude
Just because you're in a mood.
Those who are always kind
Make good friends, you will find
If they are there when things go wrong
You won't be sad for very long.'

Diana Mather

Why body language is important

Because we make up so much of our minds about a speaker so quickly, creating the right impression is key, and body language plays an important role in this. The way your body talks tells the audience whether they can trust you and the message you are going to deliver. Good posture, eye contact and a smile will generate a positive first impression, which will get you off to a very good start.

Body talk

Body talk can be positive or negative; there are telltale signs that reveal either confidence and competence or lack of research and preparation. These are the signals that show whether your audience sees you as an expert in your field or that you are not as confident as you would like your audience to think you are. The aim is to be able to control your audience like a conductor controls an orchestra, building them up and bringing them down to keep their curiosity and concentration alive. If you are feeling worried by lack of

preparation it will show; negative body language has a way of seeping out of your mind and into your body. This 'seepage' or 'leakage' will show so try to think positive thoughts and see the presentation or speech as going really well. This can be easier said than done, but thinking happy and positive thoughts has a positive effect on the way your body talks so it's worth a go.

SPEAKING WITHOUT WORDS

Dancers in all genres speak with their bodies, a feat that requires a high degree of skill and fitness. Chinese Shen Yun dancers, for instance, are some of the most remarkable athletes in the world. They cannot do what they do without hours and hours of practice and an enormous amount of self-belief. They need to know that their bodies will do what they ask them to, when they ask them to – much as most of us expect our mouths to be able to utter the words we want to say to express ourselves.

POISE AND POSTURE

The way you carry yourself is really important – it goes back to that 90 per cent in three seconds rule again.

When you walk into the room or on to the stage, take confident strides – not too long or too short. Your walk should look elegant and effortless, so it is a good idea to practise; imagine a straight line and place one foot in front of the other with the toes pointing very slightly outwards just off the line. Walk to where you are going to speak and smile at your audience before you begin.

Once you've reached the spot from which you'll give your talk:

- Stand tall.
- Imagine there is a hook pulling you up to the sky.
- Put your shoulders back and let your arms hang relaxed by your sides, just behind the seams of your skirt or trousers.
- Robin Kermode suggests clenching the buttocks to stop any tremor in the legs and to help to keep you grounded.

POSITIVE SIGNALS

Good eye contact

Good eye contact with your audience is vital if you are going to build rapport.

People can always tell when you are looking at them, even if you can't see them from a stage with lights shining in your eyes! However, staring is not good either as it makes you look aggressive and the audience feel uncomfortable. Eye contact is also essential if you are to know how your audience is reacting to what you are saying.

Smiling

Smiling is the other important way to build rapport with your audience. It is a basic human message of warmth and friendliness. The smile, however, must be genuine – one that reaches the eyes, not just the mouth. If you have used the 'Three P's' – prepare, practise and perfect – it should also come from the heart.

Sitting or standing in a relaxed position

Having your hands clasped loosely on your lap while you are waiting to speak shows that you are composed and relaxed. If people are nervous, they tend to clench their fists, getting ready for fight or flight, so keeping the hands still shows that you are on top of the situation. Sitting or standing in a relaxed position when you're getting ready to speak has the same effect.

Displaying a sense of calm

Displaying a sense of stillness and self-control shows people that you are in control of yourself and your situation and gives the audience confidence that they will enjoy what you are going to say.

NEGATIVE SIGNALS

There are a large number of negative body language signals that can show stress and anxiety. These include:

- avoiding eye contact with the audience
- looking aimlessly around the room
- folding your arms
- wringing your hands
- touching your mouth
- licking or biting your lips
- scratching your head
- twisting your neck
- shrugging your shoulders
- too much throat clearing or coughing
- fiddling with your jewellery or glasses
- playing with your hair
- jingling loose change or keys in a pocket
- sitting very straight in meetings
- sitting on the edge of the chair
- lounging in a chair
- constantly moving around in the chair
- constantly blinking, which can show insecurity or nervousness

Such negative body language is nearly always caused by lack of preparation, which causes a rush of adrenaline that puts the body into the aforementioned fight or flight mode.

Avoiding eye contact with the audience

If you don't look at your audience you cannot connect with them. People can always tell if you are evading their gaze. Rubbing your eyes, meanwhile, shows tiredness or lack of conviction, and glazed eyes reveal boredom or that your thoughts are elsewhere.

Looking aimlessly around the room

While you have to include all the audience when you are speaking, darting your eyes wildly around the room or auditorium can make you look as though you are trying to escape – which, if you are not prepared, you probably are!

Arms folded

Folding the arms across the chest is very comfortable for many people – it's a posture that means the arms are shielding one of the most vulnerable parts of the body, where the major organs are not protected by a skeleton. It also covers and protects the celiac/solar plexus or gut, also known as the 'second brain', where people often feel emotions. However, it is known as a barrier position because it can imply arrogance, vulnerability or nervousness, so should be avoided if possible.

Wringing your hands

Wringing of the hands also reveals anxiety and uneasiness, indicating uncertainty about what you are going to say, which undermines confidence and competence.

Touching your mouth and licking or biting your lips

Touching your mouth can be an indication that you are ill at ease. When someone is nervous the saliva goes from the mouth as they get ready to run from whatever it is that is frightening them. The same is true when someone is continually licking or biting their lips.

Scratching your head

Head scratching usually means that someone is tense – a state that can result in a change in body temperature, which can make the scalp feel itchy.

Twisting your neck

A lot of tension builds up in the neck when you are anxious. Twisting your neck will

help ease any tension, but it also shows everyone else that you are feeling uncomfortable.

Too much throat clearing or coughing
Throat clearing or coughing also indicates nervousness; it is caused by the saliva in the mouth drying up and the throat going into nervous spasm.

Fiddling with your jewellery or glasses
Anything that distracts from what you are saying is bad news as it is difficult enough to get your message into people's hearts and minds without them gazing at your moving hands.

Playing with your hair
The same goes for playing with your hair. Often, people are unaware of different habits, so if you know you might be tempted to constantly mess with your hair, make sure you keep it off your face.

Jingling loose change or keys in a pocket
Again, the message is what is important and if people are wondering what it is you are playing with in your pockets, they will not be listening to you.

Sitting on the edge of the chair in meetings
Sitting ramrod straight on the edge of the chair is another sign of apprehension due to lack of preparation. Try to sit up straight towards the back of the chair, but in a natural position.

Lounging in a chair
The opposite of sitting up very straight is the sprawl or lounge. This usually shows false confidence, is disrespectful and can put a barrier between you and the people you are speaking to.

What are inborn and absorbed actions?

1 **Inborn actions** are those that we do naturally – things we are not necessarily taught. Babies, for instance, have the inborn action of feeding as soon as they are born. Smiling and frowning, too, are inborn actions that are common in all cultures – they are not learned or copied behaviours. We know this because blind and deaf babies smile and frown at pertinent times and deaf babies also cry, even though they have never heard a cry. Other actions and traits can be inborn, too. For example, some people are naturally more outgoing and sociable than others; it is part of their inborn actions.

2 **Absorbed actions** are learned from those around us. Often, family members have the same mannerisms, which they have picked up at a very young age. This means that a fear of speaking in public may stem from a natural fear of making a fool of yourself or could be an absorbed action learned from a parent or older sibling. If, however, you had role models who were very extrovert, standing up and speaking might be a real pleasure for you.

Constantly moving around in the chair
Shifting about in the chair is often construed as a sign of boredom or impatience, or that you need the toilet!

Chapter 7

Conquering nerves

'The best way to conquer stage fright is to know what you are talking about.'

Michael H Mescon

It's quite natural to get nervous when you stand up to speak. In fact, you *should* feel some nerves, however experienced you are, as no nerves can lead to a rather flat and lacklustre presentation or talk. However, your nerves must be kept under control in order for you to perform well. So, how do you go about doing this? The answer is that we have to ditch the ego. It's not about you, it's about your message, so the sooner you can concentrate on delivering that rather than worrying about yourself the easier you will find the thought of presenting in public.

What makes us nervous?

Nerves are usually caused by two things: 1) lack of preparation and 2) the fear of looking stupid, the latter of which also comes back to inadequate preparation and insufficient rehearsal time. However, sometimes this insecurity goes way back to childhood or school. If someone is constantly told to keep quiet and made to feel that their point of view doesn't matter when they are young, it starts to build a natural trepidation of speaking out. If at school a teacher or other students constantly ridiculed what you had to say, this experience will make you think twice in the future before offering an opinion. These are inbuilt fears that are very real and have to be taken seriously.

Having identified and acknowledged the root cause of the fear, though, it's time to take action. And the only way to lose your nerves about performing in public is to do it, so find suitable occasions to speak. Go and seek out opportunities in a safe environment, such as speaking at a family celebration or giving a vote of thanks at work. The more you do it, the easier it will become.

Self-esteem

Self-esteem is very important. It is more than just confidence; it is how you think about and value yourself. Low self-esteem can affect how you think when you stand up and speak, so building your self-esteem is vital if you want to be able to deliver a speech well.

A large portion of self-esteem is affected by our perception of our body image. Unfortunately, society still puts pressure on both women and men to look a certain way – thinner, younger,

beautiful, gym-honed. While of course many people are happy to be themselves rather than aspiring to the perfect image seen in a magazine or on social media, there is undoubtedly a link between social media and low self-esteem, especially for younger people. I will be talking about things you can do to remedy this later in the chapter.

Happily, the story in a professional sense is somewhat more positive, especially for females. Today, the glass ceiling in many companies has almost disappeared and women can undertake most jobs that men can do. Far more women also speak in public than they used to. This is a great progression, especially since surveys show that overcoming shyness can be more of a challenge for women than men. To combat this shyness – as for fear and low self-esteem – create opportunities to get up and speak. That way you'll become so familiar with your voice and body, as well as your message, that you will actually begin to enjoy it!

Don't bottle out!

Some people will do almost anything to get out of speaking in public! This is such a shame as it means missed opportunities, especially at work. With the growth of the internet, audio and video presentations online offer great opportunities to spread your message to a huge, diverse audience across the world. However, if those presentations are unprofessional, dull and lacklustre, they will not have the clout to make a decent impact.

TED's Chris Anderson talks about the importance of presentation literacy. 'We live in an era where the best way to make a dent on the world may no longer be to write a letter to the editor or publish a book. It may be simply to stand up and say something.' I agree, presentation literacy should be taught in schools. To give children from an early age the confidence to be able to stand up and say something, to help them present a message with energy and passion is hugely important.

Create opportunities to speak

Here are a few ideas to help you take that first step towards standing up and being heard:

- ■ Speak as much as you can at school and university.
- ■ Take part in debating societies.
- ■ Join groups such as Toast Masters, Breakfast Clubs etc.
- ■ Offer to make a short speech at a family celebration, or raise a toast at a special meal.
- ■ Offer to talk to pupils at your children's school about an area in which you have expertise.

WHAT EXCUSES DO YOU MAKE FOR NOT SPEAKING?

'I can't do this.'
Yes you can! With the proper research and thorough preparation, you CAN do it!

'I don't like my voice.'
Work on your voice using the exercises in Chapter 6. Record and listen to your voice so that you get to like and appreciate your wonderful instrument of communication.

'I will forget everything I want to say.'
No you won't – not if you prepare thoroughly and rehearse the speech at least 12 times in full, before friends and family if possible for a couple of these. I know I have mentioned this a number of times now, but preparation really is the key to success.

'I may look silly.'
You won't look silly if you know how your body talks. Knowing what you are going to say means your body will do what you want it to do. Rehearse in front of a full-length mirror and then video yourself speaking until you are quite sure you are happy with what you see.

'I will let everyone down.'
You would not have been asked to speak if you were not the right person with the right ability, so have confidence in yourself and prepare, practise and perfect!

'Is my message any good?'
Put yourself in your audience's seats and ask yourself the questions you think they would ask. Then do your research, write the talk, read it and record it. Listen carefully to ensure that the message is clear, interesting and as absorbing as possible.

'I am not the right person to do this.'
If you have been asked to do it then you are the right person; you wouldn't have been asked otherwise.

'I will get too embarrassed.'
Embarrassment is a distinct emotional state and is usually brought about when we transgress social norms or are unsure of ourselves. Smiles with lips not eyes, lowering of the head, lowering of the eyes and blushing all denote embarrassment, but the Three P's will help you avoid all of these symptoms.

Living with your nerves

All actors, singers and performers suffer from a variety of nerves. In fact, some are physically sick before every performance. Feeling nervous is perfectly natural and some nerves can be a good thing, as I mentioned before. Fear gives you energy as long as you can forget about yourself and concentrate on your message. If you let yourself feel like a failure you will fail, so think like a winner.

Once you have accepted a request to speak, it is essential that you are on top form, so eat, sleep and take some exercise. The night before, try to eat some carbohydrates such as pasta or rice as they can help boost serotonin and tryptophan as well as raising blood sugar quickly, which helps you to sleep, especially if eaten about four hours before

bedtime. Exercise will help burn off any excess adrenaline.

Nervous tension can build up in the throat causing tension in the vocal cords, but doing the exercises in Chapter 6 will help to warm up your voice. A little humming in the car if you are driving to the venue will also help.

Understanding your nerves

Understanding why you feel the way you do can go a long way towards helping to alleviate the problem. Ask yourself these questions:

- Why am I tired?
- Why am I stressed?
- Why do I feel nervous?

Let's look at these one by one.

WHY AM I TIRED?

If you have been working late, taking the kids to play sports and travelling a lot then you are bound to feel tired. I find that once I know the reason why I am tired or stressed I immediately feel a bit better, because I know there is usually something I can do about it. For instance, try to eat well and take some exercise to help clear your head. Yoga and mindfulness classes will restore energy levels and help you sleep. Good sleep is essential and requires you to set a digital sunset; instead of sitting down to watch TV or playing games on your device, go to bed slightly earlier than normal at least three days a week.

WHY AM I STRESSED?

Picture the scenario: you know you have a speech to write and deliver but you haven't got time to research and prepare properly. Don't panic. You often know much more

than you think you do when it comes to your talk, so just create some 'you' time and make sure everyone knows it is blocked off and you aren't to be disturbed. Lock yourself away and start to write the speech. Don't answer the phone or the doorbell, just immerse yourself in the message and write.

WHY DO I FEEL NERVOUS?

You have always been nervous about speaking in public because it never seems to go quite the way you want it to. Your speech will only go as well as you want it to if you put in the time it needs to make it do just that, so make the time, know your stuff and the nerves will disappear.

Exercises to help banish nerves

Mindfulness or yoga classes can help you focus and empty your mind of negative thoughts. Maureen Oakden is a mindfulness and yoga practitioner who has this to say: 'Stress puts pressure on all our bodily functions. Mindfulness works by alleviating the body's stress response. It works by focusing on the breath and body movement, directing us away from sympathetic drive (fight or flight) to parasympathetic drive (calm and resting).' The body is an amazing machine and when it perceives danger it responds by producing chemicals and neuronal messages to ready us to fight or flee. In our lives today the 'dangers' we perceive are usually deadlines, social media, public speaking and other non-lethal 'threats', but your body doesn't know that these 'dangers' are not real so it sends the alert signals and chemicals to protect you, causing surges in the stress chemical cortisol, which in the long term can be damaging. 'Mindfulness trains us to recognise what is happening in our body,' says Maureen, 'and how to calm it down. Mindfulness and yoga increase body and mind awareness in ways no other practices can do.'

Using a mantra also helps to calm nerves. There are lots of apps available with different affirmations to encourage confidence and positive thinking. Examples include simple mantras such as 'Every day in every way, my speech is getting better' or 'If I think I can – I can; if I know I can – I will.' They say it takes 30 days to change someone's mindset, so it follows that if you say these mantras at least three times a day for 30 days, they can be amazingly effective.

It is, however, vital to think positive thoughts about life in general, not just about speaking in public. Optimism is very powerful; it comes from the Latin word optimum meaning 'best'. If you want to be the best, which I am sure you do, assume the best in any situation and visualise the best outcome for your talk. There is no doubt that what we think affects the way we behave. According to the Law of Attraction, the more you think you are likely to make a mess of your talk, the more likely you are to attract failure. Likewise, the more you envisage success the more you will relax, be yourself and be able to enjoy talking to people who have come to hear and enjoy what you have to say.

It helps if you can develop 'the attitude of gratitude'. Be grateful for everything you have in life. It may sound like a platitude, but the more you appreciate your health, your family, your friends, your job, the more it will help to put public speaking into perspective and encourage you to be grateful for being given the opportunity to speak.

Chapter 8

Creating confidence

'The human brain starts working the moment you are born and never stops until you stand up to speak in public.'

George Jessel

> *'Each time we face our fear, we gain strength, courage, and confidence in the doing.'*
>
> **Theodore Roosevelt**

The reasons why a person may lack confidence can be complex. As mentioned, a lot of what shapes us goes back to childhood. However, once you understand your feelings, it is possible to leave negative thoughts behind and to have confidence in yourself; if you don't, you won't succeed. Be positive, believe in yourself! Try to picture the best outcome of the situation. If you think you are going to fail, you probably will. Try to make yourself look forward to the talk or presentation and visualise success beforehand.

Positive thinking

Be positive, because the way you talk to yourself influences your neurobiological response to what you say. Positive thoughts and positive visualisation play a huge part in creating confidence. To be able to rehearse forthcoming events mentally and to have the power to dream of a successful outcome will help all of us if we truly believe we can do it. 'Without this playing with fantasy no work has ever yet come to birth. The debt we owe to the play of imagination is incalculable,' says Carl Jung.

Successful sports people commonly visualise their tactics and how they will achieve success, and so must you when preparing to speak in public. If you think positive thoughts and visualise positive outcomes the universe will usually come to your aid. If we remember that everything around us, including ourselves, is made up of atoms and every atom is a little vibration, it means that we are all vibrational by nature. In his book *Good Vibes, Good Life* Vex King talks about the Law of Vibration. 'Based on the principle of Law of Vibration, to attract good vibes we must project good vibes. As transmitters and receivers of vibrational frequencies, the vibrations we

> *'We are what we are because of the vibrations of thought which we pick up and register, through the stimuli of our daily environment.'*
>
> **Napoleon Hill**

put out are always pulling in stuff that's vibrating at a similar frequency to us.' So, if you send out positive vibes to the universe, you will receive ideas or emotions to feel positive about.

This is also true when you send out negative vibes as negative feelings lead to negative actions, which then lead to negative consequences. American semanticist S.I. Hayakawa said: 'Notice the difference when a man says to himself "I have failed three times" and what happens when he says "I am a failure".' If you tell yourself you are a failure you engender feelings of incompetence and worthlessness, but if you say you have failed three times, it means you are visualising more opportunities and therefore your feelings are more positive. When you can see things as a challenge rather than a problem, you've spun your response into a positive one.

Believe in yourself

'If you think you can do a thing or think you can't do a thing, you are right,' said Henry Ford. There is so much truth in that simple phrase. If you think you can make

a scintillating, inspirational speech, you will. The documentary *The Human Brain* claims that we say between 300 and 1,000 words to ourselves per minute, so let's make them mostly positive. Some claim that doing so can make you smarter, improve your memory and help you focus. Indeed, the US Navy SEALS instruct recruits to be mentally tough and speak positively to themselves, since this helps them to learn how to override fears resulting from the limbic brain system, a primal part of the brain that deals with anxiety.

Don't confuse memory with facts

Your memory doesn't always store information exactly as it's portrayed to you. We all tend to extract the essence of the experience and store it in ways that make the most sense to us. It's for this reason that different people seeing the same thing often give dissimilar accounts. So, accept that your memory does not always provide you with accurate information. What's more, if you have low self-esteem, your brain is inclined to store information that confirms your lack of confidence and so that is all you remember about a specific event. Go back to a negative memory that is full of self-limiting beliefs and try to get a more accurate perspective. If possible, have a chat to other people who might have another view, because things are not usually half as bad as you think they were.

False confidence

Some people will say 'fake it until you make it', by which they mean that if you do something enough times, with a certain amount of confidence even if you aren't fully proficient to start with, you'll eventually

Find your balance

A good exercise for self-belief is to stand on one leg for 30–60 seconds. This can be quite difficult if you are not used to it, so concentrate on a spot on the wall and tell yourself you *can* do it and you will be able to. I often practise this when I am waiting for a pan or the kettle to boil as it is good for balance, which in turn is good for centring oneself, which is essential when you are going to speak.

genuinely be able to do it. This can help develop confidence in the short term, but beware that people can usually tell if your confidence is fabricated – i.e. that you are faking it. Such false confidence can also be mistaken for arrogance, which isn't something you want to portray.

Interestingly, it's insecure people who often betray false confidence, confusing confidence with presumptuousness. Another way that people betray false confidence is by building themselves up and putting others down, which simply isn't cool. If you are truly confident and

happy with yourself, you will always want to give others confidence, too.

Extreme behaviour or forms of dress can also indicate false confidence, although it is worth noting that many people with a zany dress sense are

'Be yourself; everyone else is already taken.'

Oscar Wilde

extremely happy in their own skin, so don't jump to conclusions.

How to create confidence before the presentation

There are a number of ways you can create confidence before you go on stage or stand up:

- Design a mood board. This can act as a constant visual reminder of what you want to achieve. Images, scraps of speeches, affirmations, good luck charms – anything you like can all be part of your board. Put it somewhere prominent: above your desk, above your bathroom mirror, on the kitchen fridge – wherever you can see it easily. Look at the board every day and

concentrate on what the images mean to you. Note: you must truly believe that your goals are obtainable, otherwise they won't be.

■ Put your speech into perspective and have confidence in your ability to research your topic, digest the information and tell your story. And if you think of your speech as a story with a beginning, a middle and an end, you will find it easier to write it and easier to perform it.

■ Once you know you are going to speak, try keeping a diary. Jot down ideas as they come to you, then allot the amount of time you are going to need to write the talk, and how and when you are going to rehearse it. Write down the reasons why people will enjoy your talk and want to hear what you are going to say then write a list of positive points. The list could look something like this:

1 I have prepared thoroughly.
2 I know my subject.
3 I have experienced the situations I am going to talk about.
4 I know my voice sounds OK.

5 I have delivered the talk to family or friends.

6 They liked it and so will my audience!

When rehearsing your speech, make sure you are somewhere comfortable. I often go through my talks in the shower or bath, or when I go for a walk. Remember that it is very flattering to be asked to speak and nobody will ask you if they think you are not up to it.

How to maintain confidence while speaking

A strong beginning and a powerful ending to your presentation are essential for maximum impact – and this is not just the words you say but the way you say them. It is therefore a good idea to memorise the opening and the closing few lines. This will give you confidence as you will get off to a good start and know you will have a good ending.

Another way to calm nerves is to find 'friends' in the audience. Make sure you don't latch on to one sympathetic-looking person, though – find at least three or four faces you can interact with in different parts of the room or auditorium. Then, when you have relaxed, you can give the whole audience your full attention.

Don't worry if things go wrong. I knew of an eminent professor who had a rather idiosyncratic way of delivering his lectures to his students. He would walk several steps forwards and then several steps backwards with his eyes half closed as he enthusiastically deliberated his points. This particular auditorium, though, was not his usual venue and had steep steps running up the back of the stage. To the students' horror, they could see him edging nearer

Be your own cheerleader

Look at yourself in the mirror every morning and tell yourself that you are going to have a good day. It may sound like Pollyanna, but it does work. Tell yourself that you are looking good and that you are feeling happy. If you can learn to be happy in your own skin, you will have achieved what many people never do, and you will find that you are more contented and life becomes full of opportunities.

Prepare your body

Keep hydrated: drink a full glass of water before you start and make sure that you eat something. A rumbling tummy will do nothing for your confidence.

If you are feeling very nervous, a walk or some exercise is a good idea as this helps get rid of excess adrenaline. I run on the spot for a few moments if I feel there are too many butterflies doing cartwheels in my stomach.

and nearer to the steps and finally he lost his footing and disappeared out of sight, only to reappear almost immediately, still speaking without having drawn breath. Carrying on in such a situation takes a huge amount of confidence and shows that if you aren't embarrassed by falling down the stairs, your audience won't be either!

First impressions

As already discussed, we make up 90 per cent of our minds about someone in approximately 30 seconds, so creating a strong and dynamic first impression is vital

Key points for confident presentation

To create and maintain confidence both before and during the talk:

- **Be enthusiastic** – enthusiasm is a very infectious emotion and makes all the difference to how your message is received.
- **Be focused** – keep your focus on the message and the audience who will hear it.
- **Be determined** – determination to succeed means you will succeed in writing and delivering the speech you will be proud of.
- **Be patient** – Rome wasn't built in a day. It takes time to become a good presenter, but practice and preparation will get you there.

and can make all the difference to how you are perceived as a presenter. A confident first impression transmits trust and credence in what you are going to say right from the start of your talk. This puts your listeners at ease, which means that they are much more likely to pay attention. Confidence is infectious, as is a lack of confidence, so make sure you go out there with all guns blazing.

You are what you wear

What you wear has a big impact on creating the right first impression, so choose something that you like, you know looks

good and is comfortable. Anything too tight, too long or too short can make you feel self-conscious, which will erode confidence levels. You would be surprised by how critical people can be if your presentation is slightly lacklustre and their minds have time to wander. When I read the news for the BBC I got more letters from viewers saying that they did or didn't like my clothes or my hair than I did on how I presented the news! Here are a few tips and guidelines:

- If you are giving a work presentation, make sure your style of dress suits your company and the subject of your speech. If you are talking about organisational change or redundancies, sober colours and simple styles are best as you don't want to appear frivolous or insensitive. If you are talking about something creative or artistic, wear something that shows that creativity.

- If you are speaking as 'you', let your personality rip.
- Women tend to attract more scrutiny than men, especially from other women, so if you don't want to draw attention to yourself and thus take the focus away from what you are saying, don't show too much flesh – be it cleavage or leg! Angela Merkel always wears the same type of suits, but with different-coloured jackets so people don't bother to talk about her clothes. Hillary Clinton also wears outfits that don't take the attention away from her message.
- If you are on the short side, don't wear a long jacket as it will make you look smaller. Baggy or wide trousers will also shorten the legs. Studies have shown that looking taller gives us more authority, so a long, slim line is considered good.

Often bearing historical and cultural connotations, certain colours are

associated with particular feelings and emotions. For instance, colour defines seasons and ceremonies in many cultures; red and green are synonymous with Christmas and Chinese New Year. Colours can also affect how we feel subconsciously, so by making a conscious choice to wear one and not the other we can affect both our own and onlookers' moods. It is worth noting, though, that sometimes the emotions colours create are conflicting and can signify disparate phenomena, such as danger, tranquillity, wisdom or wealth, so it is worth thinking carefully if you are going to use colour as a communication tool.

Let's look at some of the most common colours and their meanings:

- ■ **Red** is stimulating and draws attention. It also says passion, excitement, danger or blood. Red inspires desire and has a strong link to sexuality. In Chinese culture, red represents luck and prosperity. So, you can wear red when you want to get pulses racing and to inspire action, but use it carefully as it can also evoke feelings of aggression.

- ■ **Orange** conveys encouragement, excitement, warmth and enthusiasm. It borders on red and can remind us of blood, but it also borders on gold and the ascent of the sun, which means that it radiates fire and warmth. It can also be a warning as it can symbolise life and death. Orange is a motivating colour and often appeals to young people. However, the negative undertones include exhibitionism and self-indulgence.

- ■ **Yellow** is the colour of optimism and conveys youthful, vigorous energy. It is similar to gold, which means 'everlasting'. Some of the most valuable things in life are gold and in

China only the emperors were allowed to wear the colour. Gold or yellow also spell wisdom and success alongside aging, as the skin and teeth can turn yellow as we get older. It is also said that yellow stimulates the left side of the brain, and therefore helps clear thinking and decision-making. It can be seen from a greater distance by the human eye than any other colour, which is why it is often used for road signs – and by those who wish to stand out in a crowd.

■ **Green** is a calming colour. It conjures up nature, growth, abundance and plenty, but can also mean jealousy and decay. In the theatre, many actors are superstitious about wearing green on stage. There are a couple of reasons for this. One is that the original stage lighting was quicklime, which had a greenish glow, meaning that actors wearing green became invisible. The other was that the actor and playwright Molière was wearing green while performing on stage in 1673 when he suffered a haemorrhage and subsequently died.

■ **Blue** is another calming colour. It implies serenity, peace and cleanliness, which is why many hospital clinics have blue walls. Cool blue is associated with conservatism and can also be perceived as aloof.

■ **Pink** is usually linked to femininity, sensitivity and love. It has associations with kindness and happiness, hence the saying 'seeing the world through rose-tinted glasses'. However, too much pink in a business setting can lead to people not being taken seriously.

■ Red and blue combine to create **purple**, which implies royalty, riches, luxury, wealth, power and wisdom. It is also the colour of spirituality. However, too much use of purple can portray over-importance and arrogance.

■ **Brown** evokes the earth, the outdoors and comfort – probably because chocolate is brown! Solidity is the message that emanates from brown; it can be a bit dull, but it shows quiet confidence and can be warm and reassuring.

■ **Grey** is considered to be unemotional and conservative, a colour trying to avoid attention. It can convey gloom and depression, but it also has a soothing effect as it is neutral. Grey is also linked with maturity and is seen as being reliable and practical. It might not be considered a glamorous colour, but grey can be very elegant and smart.

■ **Black** suggests death and mourning. It is the colour of mystery and sometimes conjures up images that are frightening and evil. A strong and powerful colour, it

also symbolises power, style and class and can be formal, sophisticated, sexy and secretive.

- ■ **White** expresses purity, innocence and youth as well as clarity, reflection and sterility.

So, what do you want to do with this knowledge? The first thing is to decide whether or not you are going to use it. Again, ask yourself who you are talking to, where is the venue, what is your message? Decide what impression you want to make and then choose your colour.

Hair and make-up

We have talked about clothes, so I am now going to concentrate on hair and make-up. It is a fact that women are judged more on hair and certainly make-up than men, although more men wear some sort of make-up too these days.

If you are speaking on a stage and there are big screens behind you, sometimes your face will fill those screens, so it is important that your hair is tidy. Why? Because if there are stray pieces of hair floating about it can take people's attention away from the message you are trying to get across.

The same applies to make-up and skin care. Check the lights before you go on stage. If they make you look pale, apply blusher. If you look tired and wan, it can raise subconscious questions about the validity of your message. Don't try anything new just before you are going to speak a different brand of make-up could cause an allergic reaction. Beware doing anything that could affect your appearance. I had a friend who went for a swim before speaking at a conference. She had dyed her hair the day before and unfortunately the chemicals in the pool turned her auburn locks a muddy shade of green.

Chapter 9

Performance

'We are what we repeatedly do. Excellence, then, is not an act, but a habit.'

Aristotle

Once you have prepared your speech the next job is to deliver it, or I would say 'perform it' as any talk should be a performance.

Sir Ken Robinson says, 'People should do whatever makes them comfortable on stage and helps them to relax. If memorising works, they should do that. It doesn't for me. One of my priorities in giving a talk is to establish a personal relationship with the audience, and to do that I want room to improvise.' It doesn't matter whether it is a handful of people in a small room or thousands in a huge auditorium, it is crucial to talk with or to people, not at them. Sir Ken may not memorise his talks, but he plans them carefully and thoroughly. When he walks on stage he knows what he wants to have said before he walks off again. It is important to bear in mind that however

many times you have spoken before, especially when using the same talk, the audience that day is new and their needs and expectations are different.

Introduce yourself if no introduction has been made

It is important to prepare a short introduction if you are not being introduced when you get up to speak. Have it ready so that you are not fazed if you are suddenly expected to start from cold. You just need to give your name and what you are going to talk about. Pause, smile, then off you go.

Where and how to stand

I advise people to stand when they are giving anything but a very informal talk. If you are standing, people must look up to you, and psychologically that gives

you an advantage. Even in informal meetings it is a good idea to stand up, as it will help you overcome the natural vulnerability that we all feel when we are the focus of attention. And that is what you need to be: the centre of attention. In order to get people to listen to you, the whole attention should be focused on you.

Find your physical focus

As discussed in earlier chapters, posture is very important when it comes to

> ### 'Nothing is more revealing than movement.'
> **Martha Graham**

performance. Although public speaking is not acting, you are 'performing' when you speak to an audience. The minute you walk on to the stage you will be consciously and subconsciously scrutinised. Being 'centred' is essential. What do I mean by that? It means having your focus on your centre of gravity. The author and hypnotist Paul McKenna tells of

Attention-stealing smartphones

Don't overlook the lure of smartphone. If you let your audience's attention wander those phones will come out of a pocket or a bag like a rabbit from a hat, so you only have about a minute to enthral people with what you are saying before they turn to alternative forms of entertainment.

meeting an Aikido (a defensive Japanese martial art) expert at an exhibition. He described Aikido as using an opponents' energy against them while remaining centred yourself. The man was small and slight and asked Paul to push him over. Paul gave the man a gentle push and knocked him off balance. Then he asked Paul to push him again. This time, no matter how hard he tried, no matter that the man was a lot shorter than him, Paul could not move him. After a while he gave up and asked the man how he did it. He explained that when we move our attention to the centre of our body we become physically and physiologically stronger.

At a point about 5cm (2in) below your navel and halfway between your naval and your spine is the spot that the Japanese call the *hara*. They believe this is the physical centre of the body and where the life force or *chi* is stored. To locate it, Paul McKenna suggests putting your thumb on your belly button; where the thumb ends is about the right position. Move your thoughts down this centre of gravity and visualise the forthcoming presentation while concentrating on your core. If you want to make sure you are focused, ask

'*The key to good technique is to keep your hands, feet and hips straight and centred. If you are centred you can move freely. The physical centre is your belly; if your mind is set there as well, you are assured of victory in any endeavour.*'

Morihei Ueshiba, founder of Aikido

someone to gently push your shoulder. If they can easily push you off balance then you are not focused, so really concentrate. If you can stand firm, it means you are using your core properly and this will help you to become strong mentally as well as physically. What's more, someone with a low centre of gravity automatically looks convincing and powerful, which is crucial when making a positive first impression in front of an audience.

Wait for the audience to become quiet

Take your time. Don't rush into the speech. If people have their minds on other things or are having conversations they won't be listening. Wait for people to stop chatting and then assess your audience. Are they restless? Are they excited? Are they expectant? Once you have assessed the mood you can tailor your presentation to meet their expectations.

TIPS TO IMPROVE PERFORMANCE

There are certain tricks and tips you can use to help your performance:

THREE S'S
1   **Stop** – before you start. This allows the brain and the mouth to get in gear.
2   **Smile** – this breaks the barrier between you and the audience. It reassures them that they are in safe hands when it comes to the information they are going to hear.
3   **Start** – only when your nerves have steadied and your heart rate has slowed down to something like normal.

THREE E'S
1   **Energy** – comes from being thoroughly prepared, knowing what you need to say and wanting to say it.
2   **Enthusiasm** – if you are not enthusiastic about your subject, then why should anyone else be? Enthusiasm will carry your audience with you and make them as interested as you are in what you have to say.
3   **Enjoyment** – this comes from having the right mindset and seeing the chance to speak as a great opportunity. If you have prepared thoroughly you can look forward to the pleasure of giving a talk.

Look at the audience

It is a natural human urge to want to look at the object we are talking about, but if you have done your research and know about the item in the glass case or on the PowerPoint screen then you don't need to keep checking. Keeping the object behind you, facing the audience, making eye contact and smiling makes it easy for your audience to relax and focus on listening.

You also need to cast your gaze evenly across the room. The importance of this was demonstrated by Dr John Kershner from the Ontario Institute of Studies in Education, who recorded teachers every 30 seconds for 15 minutes. For the most part when speaking they spent 44 per cent of the time looking at students in front of them, 39 per cent at students on their left and 17 per cent looking at students on their right. Students sitting on the left-hand side did better than those on the right, which suggests that it is important to speak to all parts of the audience equally.

Put passion into your presentation

You have to believe in what you are saying with total conviction before you can speak with passion. Some of the dictionary definitions of passion are 'strong emotion, ardour, excitement, fervour'. Think of these

> *'It's a lack of faith that makes people afraid of meeting challenges, and I believe in myself.'*
>
> **Muhammad Ali**

Be a motivating force

Motivation and inspiration are essential if you want to change people's hearts and minds. To motivate anyone, you must totally believe in your message and really want to tell it. It has to be delivered with passion and conviction and it should burst from you like a flame via your voice and your body. Put everything you have got into your delivery'.

words when you write your speech and again when you perform it.

However, it is not just your words and your voice that evoke passion; your body has to portray it, too. If you feel strongly about your message it shows in your body language, as discussed in Chapter 6. Moving around when you talk can be very effective if the movements are driven by passion. When we want people to take on board what we are saying, we automatically move towards them. Our hands also tend to move towards them, almost imploring them to hear us. Beware, though, because moving around when you are not sure what you are saying evokes a very different image – one of insecurity and uncertainty.

There are some very good speeches and speakers on YouTube, so I would advise you to look at different speakers and learn from them. However, always bear in mind that it is no good trying to imitate someone else; your style must be your own.

Use your voice

When speaking in public, if you are not using a microphone, speak clearly and a

PRACTICE POEMS

In order to practise the Five P's, read these three poems aloud. First, mark the places where you need to breathe. Start off whispering the pieces, then gradually increase the volume. Be aware of how your lips, mouth and tongue feel. Next, read them as if you are feeling sad, and then again as if you are very happy. Now try reading them with no expression. Record yourself so that you can listen back carefully and hear the difference.

THE FIRST DAY

'I wish I could remember the first day,
First hour, first moment of you meeting me:
If bright or dim the season, it might be
Summer or winter for aught I can say.
So unrecorded did it slip away.
So blind was I to see and to foresee,
So dull to mark the budding of my tree
That would not blossom yet for many a May.'
Christina Rossetti

LEISURE

'What is this life if full of care
We have no time to stand and stare?
No time to stand beneath the boughs
And stare as long as sheep and cows.
No time to see, when woods we pass
Where squirrels hide their nuts in grass.
No time to see, in broad daylight
streams full of stars, like skies at night.
No time to turn at beauty's glance
And watch her feet, how they can dance.
No time to wait till her mouth can
Enrich that smile her eyes began.
A poor life this if, full of care,
We have not time to stand and stare.'
WH Davies

SONG FOR THE WORLD

'Please save our world
Cherish our world
It's time to shout
Time's running out
Oh, hear the clock
Tick tock tick tock
Our mother earth,
Are we concerned?
What have we learned?
Please spread the word
Let your voice be heard
Join us and sing this song
It could save our world
Sing it loud everywhere
Time is running out very fast now
Time is running out very fast now.'
Diana Mather

bit louder than you would normally. Don't hurry, but vary your tone as much as possible.

FIVE IMPORTANT P'S

1 **Pace** – variations of speed.
2 **Pitch** – not too high or low. Feel comfortable.
3 **Phrasing** – think about what you are saying. Emphasise stress points.
4 **Pause** – this gives your audience a chance to absorb what you are saying and is very important.
5 **Projection** – don't shout. Produce your voice with plenty of controlled breathing.

Taking questions

When you answer questions your talk isn't over, you are still 'in the spotlight'. If it is a large audience, it's a good idea to repeat the question (although not every time) so that the rest of the audience is sure what has been asked. Look at the person who has asked the question as you start to answer and then expand it to the whole of the room, coming back at the end to the questioner.

This is a time when you can extrapolate on some points or bring in any information that you might have omitted from your speech. For example, if you are speaking without

notes and had forgotten during the main speech to make one of your most important points you can always say 'Many people ask me…' and then make the point you should have made in the talk. Don't let yourself be dragged into a debate with one particular person. If someone is very persistent and will not let a subject go, arrange to meet them afterwards.

How to cope in adverse situations

Most of the time the guests will have enjoyed good food and drink by the time you get up to speak and they should be feeling relaxed and happy. The trouble is that they can sometimes be a bit *too* happy. Nothing is worse than an audience that gets out of hand. When people have had a lot to drink they can become noisy, disorderly or even

belligerent. So, how do you cope with that? First of all, you can't compete with people talking and laughing at their own jokes and stories, so you have to be ultra-flexible and adapt your talk as best you can. Quick thinking is needed here. A good loud start can induce people to be quiet, so get a waiter to bring you a metal tray and then drop it to the floor with a crash. Another approach would be to

blow hard into the mic or to start singing in a very loud voice – desperate situations call for desperate measures! When they fall quiet, put on your best smile and say 'Now that I have your undivided attention…'

It is a shame that sometimes a few rowdy people can ruin the evening for everyone, and in extreme situations you might find that discretion is the better part of valour and you have to bring your speech to an early close.

Even if your audience is putty in your hands, there are times when speaking can become very difficult. A cough, a sore throat, a pneumatic drill in the room next door can all make your presentation a bit of a nightmare. If on the day you are to speak you find you wake up with little or no voice, you need to decide whether you think you will be able to make the speech that day or evening. Sucking throat pastilles, gargling or using a throat spray may all help, but you must decide as soon as possible whether or not you can go on in order to give the organisers time to find somebody else if necessary. For a non-business presentation there is not the same need for a particular person to give the speech. If you are the father of the bride, the chair of a committee or captain of your club, or giving a eulogy at a funeral, you could ask a close relative or friend to read for you, or have them stand by in case you start but can't finish. This is better than trying to struggle on, sounding nervous and unconfident. Teresa May experienced this first hand when she was prime minister, when she made a valiant attempt to finish a speech with a hacking cough. She got through it, but it left an impression of a woman who was reeling under the strain of the Brexit impasse.

Chapter 10

Summary and quick tips

'The true secret of giving advice is, after you have honestly given it, to be perfectly indifferent whether it is taken or not, and never persist in trying to set people right.'

Henry Ward Beecher

Basics checklist

- **The talk** – must meet its objective.
- **Information** – it needs to be clear.
- **Introduction** – should seize the attention.
- **Key points** – link them in logical order.
- **The conclusion** – make it strong and positive.
- **Team presentations** – rehearse together.
- **Visual aids** – do you need them?
- **Your laptop** – is it compatible?
- **Starting and finishing times** – stick to them.
- **Taking questions** – end on a positive note.

This chapter is a summary of what we have talked over so far. I hope you can use it as a quick steer to the information you need when you are starting to write your speech and as a guide to enable you to look up tips and advice easily and quickly when you need it.

Common errors

These are the main reasons why talks may fail in their objective or fall flat:

- Poor preparation.
- Patchy research.
- Failing to focus.
- Inadequate rehearsal time.
- Uninspiring delivery.
- Lack of confidence due to lack of preparation.

Before you agree to give a talk, ask these questions:

- Why you?
- Are you the right person?
- Why are you giving this talk?
- Are you the only speaker?
- Are you the keynote speaker?
- What time are you speaking at and for how long?
- Who else is speaking and what are their topics?
- Where is the venue?
- Is there a fee. Make sure it is worth giving up your precious time and energy.

What do you want the talk to achieve?

Once the queries above have been answered you need a clear objective. Do you want the talk to:

- Inform?
- Influence?
- Inspire?
- Sell?
- Motivate?
- Entertain?

Who are your audience?

In order to meet your objective you need to find out the following information:

- How many people will be in the audience?
- What will be their age, sex, cultural diversity?
- What are the seating arrangements?
- What job categories, positions or levels will be present?
- What is their reason for attending?
- What is the audience attitude?

Venue check

- What facilities are available?
- Is there a projector for a large audience?
- How big/dark/light is the room?
- Are there any catering arrangements?

Creation audit

Having agreed to give the talk, before you put pen to paper you should ascertain or work out:

- How much time is available?
- What is the message?
- Is it best conveyed in words or pictures?
- Is your introduction interesting enough to seize the audience's attention?
- Will the talk meet its objective?
- Are your key points in logical order?
- Have you linked each key point with the one before it?
- Have you kept everything logical and clear?
- Have you told your audience everything they need to know? (Not everything you know!)
- Have you removed any words that contradict or are repetitive?
- Have you involved your audience with the use of 'we' and 'us'?
- Have you been positive throughout?
- Is the talk written in a conversational style?
- Is the conclusion effective?
- Do you need any visual aids?
- Will they help or distract the audience?
- If the talk is very technical, would a handout be better?
- Alternatively, would handouts in addition to visual aids avoid distracting note-taking?

Visual aids

These are the visual aids you may consider using:

- ■ PowerPoint, Keynote and .. Prezi
- ■ video
- ■ audio
- ■ whiteboards
- ■ flip charts
- ■ handouts

Performance audit

When you have written, rehearsed and recorded your talk, assess the video and ask yourself:

- ■ Was your introduction powerful?
- ■ Was your message clear?
- ■ Was your topic well rehearsed?
- ■ Did you sound enthusiastic?
- ■ Did you speak too slowly?
- ■ Did you speak too quickly?
- ■ Did you come across as sincere?
- ■ Were pauses used to good effect?
- ■ Did you smile?
- ■ Did you impress, inform or convince?
- ■ Did you complement the other speakers?
- ■ Did you look relaxed?
- ■ Was the conclusion convincing?
- ■ Have you involved your audience?
- ■ Have you been positive throughout?
- ■ Was the talk delivered in a conversational style?
- ■ Did you impress, inform or convince?
- ■ Did you look relaxed?
- ■ Was the conclusion convincing?

Performance tips

FIVE IMPORTANT P'S

1 Pace
2 Pitch
3 Phrasing
4 Pause
5 Projection

THREE MORE P'S

1 Prepare
2 Practise
3 Perfect

THREE E'S

1 Energy
2 Enthusiasm
3 Enjoyment

THREE L'S

1 Look
2 Listen
3 Learn

How your body talks

POSTURE CHECK

- Stand or sit tall with your head up.
- Walk looking straight ahead with your chin parallel to the ground.

POSITIVE SIGNALS

- Good eye contact.
- Smiling.
- Nodding.
- Hands clasped loosely on the lap.
- Sitting or standing in a relaxed position.
- Displaying a sense of calm.

NEGATIVE SIGNALS

- Avoiding eye contact with the audience.
- Looking aimlessly around the room.
- Arms folded.
- Wringing the hands.
- Touching the mouth.
- Licking or biting the lips.
- Scratching the head.

Top tips

1 PEOPLE WILL LISTEN IF YOU CAN:

- show them something new
- save them time, pressure or money
- introduce a 'feel good' factor
- give them tips and hints on how to succeed
- bring in a local aspect

2 WHEN RE-PRESENTING THE SAME PRESENTATION:

- make sure the objective is still the same
- find out if there are any new speakers

3 WHEN PREPARING A SPEECH:

- refine your message
- write the talk to be said, not read
- write, read, record
- book end the talk

- Twisting the neck.
- Shrugging the shoulders.
- Too much throat clearing or coughing.
- Fiddling with jewellery or glasses.
- Playing with hair.
- Jingling loose change or keys in a pocket.
- Sitting very straight in meetings.
- Sitting on the edge of the chair.
- Lounging in a chair.
- Constantly moving around in the chair.
- Constant blinking.

Confidence checklist

Say these sentences to yourself in the mirror before you give your speech to reassure and calm yourself and instil yourself with confidence:

- I know my subject.
- I have prepared thoroughly.
- I know my voice sounds interesting.

- I have included some pertinent quotations.
- I have built in some fascinating facts and anecdotes.
- I have delivered the talk to family or friends.
- I have perfected my visual image – my clothes and make-up – to make a good first impression

Banishing nerves

- Be prepared.
- Believe in yourself.
- Practise yoga.
- Take mindfulness courses.
- Adopt mantras.

And remember: preparation is the key to confidence and confidence is the key to success!

Good luck.

Index

absorbed actions 77
adverse situations 114–15
after-dinner speeches 49
alliteration 30
anaphora 30
anecdotes 33
arms folded 75
audience 20
  age of the audience 21
  audience empathy 84
  audience research 20, 119
  diversity 23
  engaging with your audience 21
  female and male
    audiences 22–3
  how to welcome guests or the
    audience 47
  include everyone 49
  jobs or positions of the
    audience 22
  key people in the audience 23
  look at the audience 111
  size of the audience 21
  wait for the audience to become
    quiet 109
  what do they know already? 22
  what do they want to know? 21–2
audio 63

balancing exercise 93
benefit incentives 29
birthdays 53
body language 71–7
  body talk 71–2, 121
  inborn and absorbed actions 77
  negative signals 74–7, 121–3
  poise and posture 72–3
  positive signals 73–4, 121
  speaking without words 72
bottling out 82
  what excuses do you make for
    not speaking? 83
breathing for speech 69
business presentations 40–1
  repeating the presentation 41, 121

calmness 74, 95
charity events 49
chiasmus 31
clothes 99–101
  colours 101–3
conclusion 33
conferences 44

confidence 90, 123
  be your own cheerleader 97
  believe in yourself 93
  don't confuse memory with
    facts 93
  false confidence 93–5
  find your balance 93
  first impressions 98–9
  hair and make-up 103
  how to create confidence before
    the presentation 95–7
  how to maintain confidence while
    speaking 97–8
  keep calm and carry on 95
  key points for confident
    presentation 98
  pathway to success 90
  positive thinking 90–3
  power of a smile 99
  prepare your body 98
  you are what you wear 99–103
coping in adverse situations 114–15
coughing 77
cultural diversity 23

determination 98
disability diversity 23

elevator pitches 44
emphasis 69
energy 110
engaging with your audience 21
enjoyment 110
enthusiasm 98, 110
exercises to help banish nerves 86–7
expression 69
eye contact 73
  avoiding eye contact 74
  looking aimlessly around the
    room 75

fear incentives 29
fees 17
female audiences 22–3
fiddling with your jewellery or
  glasses 77
first impressions 98–9
flipcharts 62–3
focus 98
  find your physical focus 107–9
funerals 51–3
  celebrant for a day 53
  readings for funerals 51

graduation ceremonies 53
group leaders 46

hair 77, 103
hand wringing 75
handouts 63
head scratching 76

inborn actions 77
incentives 29
international conferences 44–6
interpreters 44–6
introductions 27–8, 106

jingling keys or change 77
jokes 33

key points 28–9
key words 28–9
Keynote 56–62

lips 76

make-up 103
male audiences 22–3
meetings 41–3
  sitting on the edge of the
    chair 77
  where should I sit during a
    meeting? 43
metaphors 30
mindfulness classes 86–7
motivation 111
mouth 76

neck twisting 76–7
negative signals 74–7, 121–3
nerves 80, 123
  audience empathy 84
  create opportunities to speak 83
  don't bottle out! 82–3
  exercises to help banish
    nerves 86–7
  learn from the greats 84
  living with your nerves 84
  self-esteem 80–1
  understanding your nerves 84–6
  what makes us nervous? 80
  why do I feel nervous? 86
networking groups 43–4
new technology 9

opening remarks 27–8

pace 70, 113
passion 111
pauses 70, 113
perfecting 36–7
performance 106
  be a motivating force 111
  find your physical focus 107–9
  how to cope in adverse
    situations 114–15
  introduce yourself 106
  look at the audience 111
  performance audit and tips 120
  practice poems 112
  put passion into your
    presentation 111
  taking questions 113–14
  tips to improve performance 110
  use your voice 111–13
  wait for the audience to become
    quiet 109
  where and how to stand 106–7
phrasing 70, 113
pitch 70, 113
poise 72–3
political speeches 46
positive signals 73–4, 121
positive thinking 90–3
posture 72–3, 121
power of speech 8
PowerPoint 56–62
practise 36–7
  effective practising 38–9
  practice poems 112
preparation 36–7
  prepare your body 98
  tailoring your speech to the
    event 40–53
presentations 40–1
  how to create confidence before
    the presentation 95–7
Prezi 56–62
projection 70, 113
props 16
public speaking 7–9, 12–17
puns 31

questions, taking 113–14
quotations 33

reading 37
recording 37
relevance incentives 29
retirement 49
rhetoric 30–1

scripted talks 37
self-belief 93
self-esteem 80–1
seminars 44

similes 30
sitting 74
  constantly moving around in the
    chair 77
  lounging 77
  sitting on the edge of the chair 77
slides 56
  covering your bases 60–1
  dry runs 60
  how to use slides 59–62
  make it personal 60
  transitions 61–2
  what makes a good slide? 58–9
smartphones 107
smiling 73, 99, 110
speakers 12, 36–7
  are you the right person to give
    the talk? 12
  be the best 'you' 37
  being the only or the keynote
    speaker 15
  fees 17
  how can you use your talk to
    achieve its aim? 14–15
  how to welcome guests or the
    audience 47
  several speakers 16, 46
  Three Ps (prepare, practise,
    perfect) 36–7, 120
  time and length of talk 15–16
  voice 67–70
  what do you want the talk to
    achieve? 13–14
  where is the venue? 17
  why are you giving this talk? 12–13
  writing the talk 13
standing 74, 107–8
stress 84–6

talks 12–15, 26
  basics checklist 118
  common errors 118
  creation audit 119
  importance of timekeeping 17
  props 16
  questions to ask 119
  time and length of talk 15–16
  top tips 121
team presentations 41
TED (Technology, Entertainment
  and Design) talks 16
Three Es (energy, enthusiasm,
  enjoyment) 110, 120
Three Ls (look, listen, learn) 120
Three Ps (prepare, practise,
  perfect) 36–7, 120
Three Ss (stop, smile, start) 110
throat clearing 77
timekeeping 17, 46

time and length of talk 15–16
tiredness 84
tongue twisters 68
tour guides 46
tricks of the trade 33
  rhetoric 30–1
tricolonic structures 30

useful phrases 33

venues 17
  time to stand and stare 43
  venue check 119
video 63
virtual presentations 41
visual aids 56, 120
  audio 63
  flipcharts 62–3
  handouts 63
  PowerPoint, Keynote and
    Prezi 56–62
  traditional visuals 56
  video 63
  whiteboards 62
visual language 29
voice 67, 111–13
  breathing for speech 69
  five important Ps (pace,
    pitch, phrasing, pause,
    projection) 70, 113, 120
  how to speak clearly 67–70
  tongue twisters 68
  vocal exercises 69–70

weddings 49–50
  best man 51
  bride 51
  bridegroom 50
  father or proposer of the bride 50
  readings for weddings 51
welcoming guests 47
whiteboards 62
wordplay 31
words 8
writing 13, 26, 37, 121
  conclusion 33
  golden rules 13
  jokes and anecdotes 33
  key words and key points 28–9
  opening remarks and
    introduction 27–8
  quotations 33
  rhetorical tricks of the trade 30–1
  useful phrases 33
  visual language 29

yoga classes 86–7

Zoom 41

THE AUTHOR

Diana Mather is an author, TV and radio presenter and an acclaimed coach and trainer in public speaking, presentations skills and voice. She has an international reputation for excellence and is a regular contributor to radio and television programmes, commenting on matters of style, personal presentation and international business and social etiquette.

Diana originally trained as an actor and as a former BBC newsreader and journalist, so she knows how to get to the nub of a story, which has been extremely useful when writing speeches. She has trained senior and middle management from a large number of international organisations as well as MPs from the House of Commons and House of Lords, the States of Jersey (Channel Islands) and Members of Parliament in Barbados, Trinidad & Tobago, Nigeria and Kenya, as well as members of Middle Eastern royal families.

Diana is an Export Champion for the Department of International Trade and the Northern Powerhouse in the UK, and is accredited by the Continuous Professional Development (CPD) Standards Office as a speaker.